KIPLING'S INDIA

LOOKING TOWARD KABUL

"The mountains . . . tall and black" and "bitter cold." The country of *The Lost Legion*, *The Man Who Was*,

KIPLING'S INDIA

By

ARLEY MUNSON

GYAN

Published by

Gyan Publishing House
5, Ansari Road
Daryaganj, New Delhi-110002
Phone: 011-47034999, 9811692060
E-mail: books@gyanbooks.com

Distribution Network
gyanbooks.com
India, USA, Canada, UK, Australia, France

ISBN : 978-81-212-6619-2 (PB)
First Published, 1915

2nd Impression 2022

Printed at: Gyan Press, Delhi.

KIPLING'S INDIA
Author: Arley Munson

KIPLING'S INDIA

BY

ARLEY MUNSON

AUTHOR OF "JUNGLE DAYS, BEING THE EXPERIENCES OF AN AMERICAN WOMAN PHYSICIAN IN INDIA"

Illustrated

1915

TO MY SISTERS,

MARY WOOSTER SUTTON

AND

GERTRUDE MUNSON HULST

CONTENTS

ILLUSTRATIONS

INTRODUCTION

THERE are probably many thousand readers of Rudyard Kipling who have at some time or other laid aside the particular book that happened to be in hand at the moment and asked mentally, "Just what sort of a place is this that Kipling mentions? What is its life, what are its charms, and what the reason for its existence?" The object of this work is to briefly describe these bits of India which have served as a background for Kipling's songs and stories. From Bombay, the birthplace of Kipling and the threshold of India from the West, the scribe will attempt to carry the reader in imagination first to Simla, far up on the northeastern border among the Himalaya Mountains which separate India from mysterious Thibet—the Anglo-India of Rudyard Kipling, the India of Mrs. Hauksbee and Mrs. Reiver, of the Gadsbys and of Wressley of the Foreign Office; in a word, the India of the scores of men and women who flit across the scene in the stories that make up the greater part of *Plain Tales from the Hills, Under the Deodars*, and *The Story of the Gadsbys;* on into the heart of the Himalayas where Kim and the lama and Hurree Babu "stalked" the Russian spies; thence southwest to the Great Rajputana Desert, the country of *The Strange Ride of Morrowbie Jukes,* and of Nick Tarvin of *The Naulahka;* northward again to the Border Country on the trail of Dravot and Carnehan of *The Man Who Would Be King;* and of Jakin and Lew of *The Drums of the Fore and Aft;* from the Border down through India to Burma; and along the haunting road to Mandalay. Let the reader suppose, then, for example, that he is a tourist in India—like Pagett, M. P., of the verses, though with qualifications, for "Pagett, M. P., was a liar, and a fluent liar therewith";—and that his ship has brought him into Bombay Harbour to begin his tour through Kipling's India.

KIPLING'S INDIA

I
THE THRESHOLD OF INDIA

KIPLING'S INDIA

I

The Threshold of India

EVEN before the traveller reaches the Harbour of Bombay, he hears the echoes of Kipling's words:

> The Injian Ocean sets and smiles
> So sof', so bright, so bloomin' blue,—
> There aren't a wave for miles and miles
> Excep' the jiggle from the screw;

and there steals over him the spirit of languor and mystery which belongs to this land of dreams and world-old romance.

Bombay, the metropolis of India, is dubbed by Kipling the queen of cities, and she well deserves the title, for she far surpasses all other cities of Asia in beauty and riches. In the "Song of the Cities," Bombay accurately describes herself in her address to England:

> Royal and Dower-royal, I, the Queen,
> Fronting thy richest sea with richer hands—
> A thousand mills roar through me where I glean
> All races from all lands.

The first sight of the great modern city of a million inhabitants is enchanting, as it juts out into the sea over eleven miles of ground. On the blue surface of the harbour float the ships of every nation. A few miles back from the shore rise the green slopes of Malabar Hill, and still farther back and misty blue in the distance tower the magnificent Western Ghauts. Most of the streets are wide and well kept; the city is rich in modern improvements, such as gas and plumbing and well-equipped tramcars; and it boasts of some of the most beautiful and best-constructed public buildings in the British Empire, among which the Victoria railway station, of late Gothic architecture, stands supreme. Still one is never deceived into thinking Bombay a city of the Occident. Brightly painted carts drawn by gentle, hump-shouldered bullocks are on every hand; the prevailing gayety of colour in the dress of the people is almost dazzling; and the native pedestrian is far more likely to be in the middle of the street than on the sidewalk especially provided for him.

Bombay owes most of its wealth and greatness to the Parsis, descendants of the Persians who for the sake of their religious liberty fled to the Malabar coast of India at the time of the Mahomedan conquest of Persia some eight centuries ago; and who, though less than one hundred thousand in number, practically control the philanthropic, educational, and industrial affairs of the city. The Parsi Cemetery on Malabar Hill is one of the chief places of interest to the tourist. There among beautiful groves stand the "Towers of Silence," great white, cylindrical structures, open at the top, where the Parsis deposit their dead to be devoured by the vultures which are always hovering near; this is in accordance with the command of their prophet Zoroaster that the dead must not be allowed to defile the sacred elements, earth, fire, and water.

An interesting excursion is the boat trip out to the Island of Elephanta, about seven miles distant from Bombay and containing Hindu temples excavated from the solid rock. These cave temples take high rank among the rock sculptures of the world, and are filled with columns and giant figures of gods wonderfully wrought and carefully distributed.

It was at the Apollo Bunder, a landing-place for boats in Bombay, that five-year-old "Punch-Baba" ("Baa, Baa, Black Sheep"), bade good-bye for long, long years to his life of perfect love with Mamma and Papa and the adoring Indian servants, to become in England a helpless victim of that tragedy of Anglo-Indian life, the necessary separation of children from their parents.

From Bombay, Captain Corbyn of the 141st Punjab Cavalry, "young . . . rich, open-handed, just, a friend of poor troopers, keen-eyed, jestful, and careless," with his loving and devoted friend, Umr Singh, a Sikh of highest military rank, embarked for Africa and "A Sahibs' War" (*Traffics and Discoveries*) only to meet death at the hands of cowardly assassins—the "Sahibs" who were not "Sahibs," whose treachery was so swiftly and terribly punished by Corbyn's friends and comrades, the "*Durro Muts.*"

II
ANGLO-INDIA

II

Anglo-India

As the traveller leaves Bombay for the interior in search of Kipling haunts, he naturally goes first to Simla, for "at Simla," writes Kipling, "all things begin and many come to an evil end." And before Simla comes the way to Simla. The best way to proceed from Bombay is by the Punjab Express, and the best time is April, the beginning of India's hot weather when all Anglo-India migrates to the Hills. This is not the weather for travel on the Plains; the breezes stirred up by the rush of the train seem to come from the depths of a furnace seven times heated. But the Indian railway coach is arranged to give all the comfort possible to the hot-weather traveller. The tiny dressing-room at the end of the compartment provides a cool comforting wash whenever desired, and the double roof of the coach has a projection on both sides which acts as a slight shield from the sun. Heavy shutters and stained glass in all the windows modify the glare, while in one of the windows is placed a disk-shaped curtain of scented grass which can be revolved by means of a small handle and which at each revolution dips into a concealed basin of water. The air, cooled by its passage through the wet curtain, delightfully refreshes the interior of the coach. Then, too, one is almost sure to have his coach to himself, so he may lounge as lazily as he pleases on the long, leather-cushioned seats, which, with the addition of pillow and rug, make excellent beds at night. At almost any station, he can obtain delicious tea and toast, or, by telegraphing ahead, a very good and substantial meal.

Scarcely thirty-three hours after leaving Bombay the traveller comes to Umballa, and changes there for the branch line to Kalka, for Kalka leads to Simla, the beloved, the summer capital of India, and the most fashionable summer resort in the country.

From Kalka, the little train creeps slowly upward, curving round and round the mountain for fifty-five miles. Below and almost constantly in sight lies the tonga road glistening white in the sunshine. Groups of men and drove after drove of camels climb slowly up the steep path, while tongas dash past them at a furious pace. Great cactus trees appear everywhere; then at last the pines show dark and rich and green, speaking of the higher hills; and seven hours from the time of starting, the train arrives at Simla *pahar*, seven thousand feet above the sea.

Only the Viceroy and a few other privileged ones may

SIMLA FROM THE KALKA ROAD

Of this city of the hills the Kipling of other days said, in the beginning of "The Education of Otis Yeere," a tale involving Mrs. Hauksbee and her complex philosophy: "Here begins the story where every right-minded story should begin, that is to say, at Simla, where all things begin and many come to an evil end."

drive in carriages at Simla, but there is no lack of conveyances. At the Simla station, a dozen 'rickshaw *jhampanis*, a merry, bantering group of men, rush toward the train, each *jhampani* loud in praise of his own 'rickshaw and equally loud in denunciation of the 'rickshaws of his rivals. A ride in a Simla 'rickshaw is a thrilling experience. With two of the strong, bare-legged *jhampanis* pushing and two pulling the overgrown "perambulator," it fairly spins along the smooth, narrow path. The *jhampanis*, delighted into greater recklessness by the passenger's gasps of fear and surprise, whirl him at breakneck speed around some sharp corner or down a steep path, until with an extra flourish they stop at his destination.

Peliti's Hotel is a charming place, and the traveller will do well to put up there during his stay at Simla. In general, he will find it much like other first-class Indian hotels. In the large bedrooms, the open fireplaces and the absence of mosquito curtains show him that he is in the Hills. The comfortable sitting-room invites him to read and dream in the great chairs, and the well-ordered café is of never-failing interest, for here in the groups of laughing, faultlessly dressed English men and women he finds the true Anglo-Indian. Among them the barefooted Indian waiters, in white trousers, long coats, and turbans, with wide sashes of bright-coloured silk, flit noiselessly to and fro with a machine-like devotion to their duties.

The air is fresh and bracing with just the touch of chill that makes one glad of the warmth of a light jacket; and the wild roses and honeysuckle, the soft, green grass, and the fruit trees of a temperate climate abound on every hand. But one cannot forget that he is in the Tropics, for while walking along the quiet paths, it is no unusual thing to hear a crash of branches overhead as a huge gray ape drops from the trees to the ground and scampers away on all fours. And the birds, too, are of the southland—parrots, cockatoos, and other harsh-voiced birds of brilliant plumage, and the sweet-voiced little köil, charming the ear with its song.

The pleasant cottages of the Anglo-Indians, the shops, many of which would do credit to London's greatest shopping district, the public buildings, and the hotels are placed on terraces, one above the other, all down the steep mountainside. Many of these buildings overlook the Mall, which is like a great treeless boulevard and is the social and business centre of Anglo-Indian Simla. It slopes up through the Bazaar to the Town Hall and Jakko Hill, a thickly wooded height rising a thousand feet above the town. From the broad road, five miles long, which winds round the base of Jakko, the Himalayan-Thibet Road leads off to the higher Himalayas. The great peaks, dark with pines and deodars (the Himalayan cypress), sweep off into space, range on range, until limited at last by the snowy mountains towering twenty-two thousand feet above the sea.

To the north of the town stands Elysium Hill, and six miles west of Jakko are Prospect, Observatory, and Summer hills. On Observatory Hill, and occupying the finest viewpoint in Simla, is Viceregal Lodge, the stately summer home of the Viceroy, set well back in beautiful grounds. The various Vicereines have tried to make their Simla home as English as possible, and it might be England but for the presence of the grinning little Ghurkas, the Viceroy's Guard of Honour. Still farther west, and somewhat apart, stands Jutogh Hill, occupied by a battery of artillery. Between Elysium and Summer hills is a lovely little valley, Annandale, where the beautiful Annandale roses grow and where the Simla sports are held.

English men and women are everywhere, cantering through the Mall or under Jakko on horseback, or merrily greeting one another from their 'rickshaws. Occasionally one sees Indians of high rank, and always the Indian working people. Conspicuous among them are the Government *chaprassis*, with long scarlet coats and wide scarlet and yellow belts, the special *chaprassi* of the Viceroy being distinguished from the rest by the Viceroy's coronet and monogram embroidered on the breast of his coat.

Simla was the scene of Captain Gadsby's courtship of Minnie Threegan when he transferred his attentions from "Poor, Dear Mamma" (*The Story of the Gadsbys*) to her daughter. A few weeks later came the engagement which so completely surprised Captain Gadsby's friends, who thoroughly discussed the case ("The World Without") and could scarcely believe that "old Gaddy" had been "hooked" at last.

The "Venus Annodomini" (*Plain Tales from the Hills*) was an "Anglo-Indian deity" who, for a generation, had been worshipped by all the masculine world at Simla:

> There was a legend among the Hills that she had once been young; but no living man was prepared to come forward and say boldly that the legend was true. Men rode up to Simla, and stayed, and went away and made their name and did their life's work, and returned again to find the Venus Annodomini exactly as they had left her.

When "Very Young" Gayerson joined the others in the worship of the Venus Annodomini, he

> was not content to worship placidly and for form's sake, . . . He was exacting, and, therefore, the Venus Annodomini repressed him,

and shocked his spirit by telling him that she had a daughter nineteen years old. His spirit suffered a still greater shock when he learned that she had been a sweetheart of his father's "ever so long ago." So "Very Young" Gayerson rode down from Simla and "Young" Gayerson, his father, remained and took his place at the side of the Venus Annodomini.

Ahasuerus Jenkins of the "Operatic Own" ("Army

SIMLA—THE HILLSIDE

Here are the cottages of the Anglo-Indians who are able to get away from the heat and dust storms of the Indian desert. Here was the house of Mrs. Hauksbee, the "stormy petrel," which she shared for a time with Mrs. Mallowe. Here, on three fourths Jack Barrett's monthly screw, remained Mrs. Barrett, to console the other man, and to mourn "five lively months at most," her husband's subsequent death at Quetta. Here, too, in the prehistoric days, was the little house of Delilah Aberyswith, "a lady —not too young—with a perfect taste in dresses, and a badly bitted tongue." Above and beyond are the "wooded heights of Simla" of *The Masque of Plenty*

.ead-Quarters"), in spite of his shortcomings in horsemanship and in matters military, "had a head upon his shoulders."

He took two months at Simla when the year was at the spring,
And underneath the deodars eternally did sing.
He warbled like a bul-bul, but particularly at
Cornelia Agrippina, who was musical and fat.

Cornelia "controlled a humble husband, who, in turn, controlled a Dept." so when the musical accomplishments of Ahasuerus had won Cornelia's favour, his success in the Government service was assured.

Now, ever after dinner, when the coffee-cups are brought,
Ahasuerus waileth o'er the grand pianoforte;
And, thanks to fair Cornelia, his fame hath waxen great,
And Ahasuerus Jenkins is a power in the State!

In strolling through the town on the trail of the Kipling characters, you begin at the Kalka tonga road by which Mahbub Ali and Kim (*Kim*) went up to Simla,

the wandering road, climbing, dipping, and sweeping about the growing spurs; the flush of the morning laid along the distant snows; the branched cacti; tier upon tier the stony hillsides; the voices of a thousand water-channels; the chatter of the monkeys; the solemn deodars, climbing one after another with down-drooped branches; the vista of the plains rolled out far beneath them; the incessant twanging of the tonga-horns and the wild rush of the led horses when a tonga swung round a curve; . . .

This tonga road was the scene of "As the Bell Clinks" in which a lover tells of his thoughts and emotions and of how the tonga coupling bar gave him sage advice in regard to his courtship:

It was under Khyraghaut I mused:—Suppose the maid be haughty—
[There are lovers rich—and forty] wait some wealthy Avatar?
"Answer, monitor untiring, 'twixt the ponies twain perspiring!"
"*Faint heart never won fair lady,*" creaked the straining tonga-bar.
"*Can I tell you ere you ask Her?*" pounded slow the tonga-bar.

Last, the Tara Devi turning showed the lights of Simla burning,
Lit my little lazy yearning to a fiercer flame by far.
As below the Mall we jingled, through my very heart it tingled—
The reiterated order of the threshing tonga-bar:—
"*Try your luck—you can't do better!*" twanged the loosened tonga-bar.

In "An Old Song," another lover brings his tonga road into his verse:

So long as 'neath the Kalka hills
The tonga-horn shall ring,
So long as down the Solon dip
The hard-held ponies swing;
So long as Tara Devi sees
The lights o' Simla town,
So long as Pleasure calls us up,
And duty drives us down,
If you love me as I love you
What pair so happy as we two?

THE HEART OF RUDYARD KIPLING'S ANGLO-INDIA

The Mall at Simla, with the Town Hall in the background and Jakko Hill beyond. The Thackerayan in Pall Mall or Russell Square conjures up the ghosts of the Pendennises and the Osbornes; the Dickensian in the Borough High Street searches for such stones of the old Marshalsea prison as exist to recall the figures of Little Dorrit and Arthur Clenham; the Balzacian on the Boulevards sees in imagination countless characters from the Comedie Humaine. But for the reader of the early Kipling the Simla Mall suggests not two, or ten, but a hundred men and women, Captain Gadsby and Minnie Threegan, and their best man, Jack Mafflin, Mrs. Hauksbee, and the triple intuition of the woman, her deadly rival Mrs. Reiver, Moriarty, Strickland of the police and Miss Youghal, Jack Pansay, Kitty Mannering and Mrs. Wessington of *The Phantom 'Rickshaw*, Pluffles the Subaltern, Barrsaggott, Miss Beighton, and young Cubbon, Tarrion, Peythroppe, the Cusack-Bremmils, and others too numerous for mention

Under the Tonga-Office lamps, at the end of the tonga road, Mrs. Schreiderling met the newly arrived tonga of "The Other Man" (*Plain Tales from the Hills,*) who sat

in the back seat, very square and firm, with one hand on the awning-stanchion and the wet pouring off his hat and moustache, . . . —dead.

Not far from the Tonga Office is the Public Works Office toward which Hannasyde was climbing when he met for the first time Mrs. Landys-Haggert ("On the Strength of a Likeness"). Hannasyde kept an

"unrequited attachment by him as men keep a well-smoked pipe —for comfort's sake, and because it had grown dear in the using";

and Mrs. Landys-Haggert was "the living, breathing image" of Alice Chisane, "the girl who had made him so happily unhappy." So Hannasyde made love "through instead of to" Mrs. Haggert until he learned too late that she "was not in the least like Alice Chisane, being a thousand times more adorable."

Just beyond the Public Works Office is the Post Office where the "Tertiam Quid" ("At the Pit's Mouth") and the "Man's Wife," "kittenish in her manners, wearing generally an air of soft and fluffy innocence," but "deadlily learned and evil-instructed," used to mail to the Man, "then stewing in the Plains on two hundred rupees a month (for he allowed his wife eight hundred and fifty), and in a silk banian and cotton trousers,"

a letter which said

"that she was longing for him to come up to Simla. The Tertiam Quid used to lean over her shoulder and laugh as she wrote the notes."

Then off to Annandale, always the sporting ground of Simla. In the old days when archery used to be the favourite pastime there, Kitty Beighton of "Cupid's Arrows" (*Plain Tales from the Hills*) shot her way out of her unsatisfactory connection with Barr-Saggott and into the happiness of true love.

You must surely visit Viceregal Lodge, the scene of numerous Kipling tales. It was here that Mellish, the inventor, was admitted to the honour of tiffin with the Viceroy, through the mistake of Wonder, the Private Secretary, who had intended to invite the great "Mellishe" of Madras; and here the inventor explained to the curious and half-amused Viceroy the wonders of "A Germ Destroyer" (*Plain Tales from the Hills*), which so effectually broke up the entire Viceregal household, and ended, to the intense delight and satisfaction of the Viceroy, in the departure to England of Wonder, the "masterly" private secretary, concerning whom "all

"The solemn deodars, climbing one after another with down-drooped branches"—*Kim*

SIMLA FROM THE TARA DEVI

THE ROAD DOWN ELYSIUM HILL

It was here that, in *The Phantom 'Rickshaw*, Dr. Heatherlegh decided that Jack Pansay was either mad or drunk. For five minutes Pansay, on horseback, had been talking the commonplaces of the day to the thing that was quite invisible to other eyes

Simla agreed that there was 'too much Wonder, and too little Viceroy' in that rule."

At Viceregal Lodge, Miss Haverley in "Only a Subaltern" (*Under the Deodars*), gave her heart to Bobby Wick, the young Subaltern who so thoroughly won the love and admiration of his men that when he drifted away "on the easy tide of Death," Private Dormer expressed the sentiments of everybody who had known Bobby Wick, in the emphatic words,

'——Bloomin' orf'cer? . . . Hangel! *Bloomin'* hangel! That's wot 'e is!'

The Supreme Legislative Council of India were sitting in state at Viceregal Lodge when little Tods of "Tods' Amendment" (*Plain Tales from the Hills*) broke in upon their solemn deliberations with his wild appeals for them to help him control his goat Moti who was dragging Tods, much against his will, over the lawn and across the flower beds. Tods was the small English boy who, by his familiar friendship with *jhampanis*, shopkeepers, hill-coolies, and money-lenders, was able to give valuable counsel to the Supreme Legislature of India, in regard to "The Sub-Montane Tracts *Ryotwary* Revised Enactment." From which counsel came the amendment and the consequent immense popularity of Tods among his native friends.

At a dance at Viceregal Lodge, you meet Mrs. Hauksbee, the "Stormy Petrel,"

> a little, brown, thin, almost skinny, woman, with big, rolling, violet-blue eyes, and the sweetest manners in the world, . . . clever, witty, brilliant, and sparkling beyond most of her kind; but possessed of many devils of malice and mischievousness.

She attended this special dance as the result of the clever forgery of her friend Tarrion of "Consequences" (*Plain Tales from the Hills*), for whom she won favour and fortune by her miraculous knowledge of the affairs of the mighty East Indian Government. "Three and—An Extra" (*Plain Tales from the Hills*) tells of another dance which Mrs. Hauksbee attended at Viceregal Lodge when she struggled with Bremmil's wife for Bremmil's attention and was ignominiously defeated.

Before you return to the centre of town, you should go out to Summer Hill, for in the shade of Summer Hill "went a-walking" Delilah Aberyswith—

> ———a lady—not too young—
> With a perfect taste in dresses and a badly bitted tongue,

and Ulysses Gunne, a man

> Whose mode of earning money was a low and shameful one.
> He wrote for divers papers, which, as everybody knows,
> Is worse than serving in a shop or scaring off the crows.

There Ulysses, patiently seeking the truth, "pleaded softly" with Delilah to reveal a Viceroy's important secret of which she had knowledge, for

SIMLA—VICEREGAL LODGE

The scene of numerous Kipling tales. It was here that Mellish, the inventor, so effectually broke up the entire Viceregal household with his marvellous "Germ Destroyer." (*Plain Tales from the Hills.*) At Viceregal Lodge Miss Haverley in "Only a Subaltern" (*Under the Deodars*) gave her heart to Bobby Wick, and here Mrs. Hauksbee, the "Stormy Petrel," attended more than one dance with momentous consequences

. . . perhaps the wine was red—
Perhaps an Aged Councillor had lost his aged head—
Perhaps Delilah's eyes were bright—Delilah's whispers sweet—
The Aged Member told her what 'twere treason to repeat.

So when

The wasteful sunset faded out in turkis-green and gold,
. . . that bad Delilah told!

Next morn, a startled Empire learnt the all-important News;
Next week, the Aged Councillor was shaking in his shoes;
Next month, I met Delilah, and she did not show the least
Hesitation in asserting that Ulysses was a "beast."

Retracing your steps you come again into the Bazaar and turn off to Elysium Hill. On the road leading to Elysium Hill, Heatherlegh, "Simla's best and kindest doctor," first met Jack Pansay, who was talking to the invisible occupant of "The Phantom 'Rickshaw" and down below the Ridge on which the English Church stands, on the Blessington Lower Road, Agnes saved the lives of Pansay and the Doctor.

Back to the Bazaar and down a slope to the Combermere Bridge, near the left railing of which Jack Pansay, staring with drawn white face and horror-filled eyes, saw for the first time the phantom 'rickshaw,

four *jhampanies* in 'mag-pie' livery, pulling a yellow-panelled, cheap, bazar 'rickshaw, in which sat Agnes Keith-Wessington, her handkerchief in hand, her golden head bowed on her breast, and her tremulous voice pleading,

> "Jack! Jack, darling! It's some hideous mistake, I'm sure. *Please* forgive me, Jack, and let's be friends again."

Peliti's Hotel is here and it was into Peliti's café that Pansay rushed, half fainting, to get the cherry brandy which should dispel the terrible illusion. It will be remembered that Mrs. Hauksbee and Mr. Bremmil of "Three—and An Extra" tiffened at Peliti's under the shocked gaze of the Simla public, while Mrs. Bremmil stayed at home turning over her dead baby's frocks and crying into the empty cradle. Peliti's Hotel at Simla is the place to which reference is made by the "artless *Bandar*" ("Divided Destinies"), the monkey that entered into a mortal's dream and, on various grounds, roused the mortal's envy:

> ". . . and no, never in my life
> Have I flirted at Peliti's with another *Bandar's* wife."

Just above Peliti's is Hamilton's shop where Jack Pansay bought the engagement ring for Kitty Mannering, and concerning which the *Bandar* protests to the mortal,

> "Nor do I waste at Hamilton's my wealth on pretty things."

Now, we are on the Mall where Pansay used to walk beside the phantom 'rickshaw, deep in conversation with his

ghostly Light-o'-Love . . . to the unspeakable amazement of the passers-by.

Mrs. Schreiderling, mourning vainly for her dead love, "The Other Man,"

used to trot up and down the Mall, on that shocking bad saddle, looking as if she expected to meet some one round the corner every minute.

On the Mall, "Wressley of the Foreign Office" (*Plain Tales from the Hills*) "the known, honoured, and trusted man among men," lost his heart to Tillie Venner,

a frivolous, golden-haired girl who used to tear about Simla Mall on a high, rough Waler, with a blue-velvet jockey-cap crammed over her eyes,—

the girl with a pretty lisp, the girl who did not understand.

The miraculous shop of Lurgan Sahib, Kim's mysterious friend, is on the Mall, with its collection of devil-dance masks—"horned masks, scowling masks, and masks of idiotic terror"—and "fiend-embroidered draperies of those ghastly functions"; quaint ornaments; Oriental weapons of war; and wonderful jewels.

Near the upper part of the Mall, on the slopes of Jakko, is Christ Church where Captain Mafflin, the best man, so devotedly piloted his old chum through the mysteries of the ceremony when Minnie Threegan, "Little Featherweight" (*The Story of the Gadsbys*) "not afraid with any amazement," was married to Captain Gadsby of the Pink Hussars.

In "My Rival," Sweet Seventeen gives vent to her feelings in regard to her rival, thirty-two years her senior:

She rides with half a dozen men
  (She calls them "boys" and "mashes,")
I trot along the Mall alone;
  My prettiest frocks and sashes
Don't help to fill my programme-card,
  And vainly I repine
From ten to two A. M. Ah me!
  Would I were forty-nine.

. . . .

But even She must older grow
  And end Her dancing days,
She can't go on for ever so
  At concerts, balls, and plays.
One ray of priceless hope I see
  Before my footsteps shine:
Just think, that She'll be eighty-one
  When I am forty-nine!

Here on the Mall, Strickland, disguised as "Miss Youghal's *Sais*" (*Plain Tales from the Hills*), begged his

Copyright by Underwood & Underwood, N. Y.

SIMLA—BEFORE CHRIST CHURCH

Christ Church, on the slopes of Jakko, is where Captain Mafflin, the best man, so devotedly piloted his old chum through the mysteries of the ceremony when Minnie Threegan, "Little Featherweight" (*The Story of the Gadsbys*) "not afraid with any amazement," was married to Captain Gadsby of the Pink Hussars

friend for a box of cheroots. This was our old friend Strickland of the Police, whom people did not understand and could not appreciate,

> a quiet, dark young fellow—spare, black-eyed—and, when he was not thinking of something else, a very interesting companion.

Simla Club stands on a terrace just above the Mall. It was there that Strickland, after his scene with the General, rushed into the Club in the clothes of Miss Youghal's *sais* and galloped off again with half the Club's wardrobe on his back, to the house of "Old Youghal" and happiness. The Colonel and Platte, the Subaltern, dressing in a hurry, exchanged the "Watches of the Night" (*Plain Tales from the Hills*) at the Simla Club, whereby arose a complication of circumstances which gave Mrs. Larkyn, righteously indignant with the Colonel's wife, a chance to avenge the wrongs of her friends. At the Club, you again meet Jack Pansay of "The Phantom 'Rickshaw." Here after the Doctor's explanation of "fits," Pansay recognized the fact that for the rest of his natural life he would be among but not of his fellows. It was at the Simla Club, too, that the story of "The Bisara of Pooree" (*Plain Tales from the Hills*)—"the only regularly working, trustworthy love-charm in the country, with one exception"—was told to Churton, its possessor, and overheard by Pack, "a nasty little man who must have crawled into the Army by mistake," and who was nearly mad with his absurd infatuation for Miss Hollis . . . who was good and sweet, and five-foot-seven in her tennis-shoes,

and who "looked on Pack as some sort of vermin running about the road."

"The Foundry," the cottage of Mrs. Hauksbee and Mrs. Mallowe, also overlooks the Mall. At "The Foundry," Mrs. Hauksbee "sat at the feet of Mrs. Mallowe and gathered wisdom"; and as a result, decided to undertake "The Education of Otis Yeere" (*Under the Deodars*). There, when the "education" was complete, Mrs. Hauksbee wept out her chagrin and disappointment into the sympathetic ears of Mrs. Mallowe.

In "A Second-Rate Woman" (*Under the Deodars*)—the story that gives us better than any other the noble, womanly side of Mrs. Hauksbee's nature, in her patient nursing of little Dora—"The Foundry" figures again as the scene of little Dora's peril. With the child choking to death, and her mother and Mrs. Hauksbee helpless with fright, the "Dowd" stepped in, with cool head and steady hand applied the saving medicine, and received the remorseful embraces of Mrs. Bent and Mrs. Hauksbee. Over the teacups at "The Foundry," Mrs. Hauksbee proved that she "was sometimes nice to her own sex," when, for the sake of an English girl whom she had never seen, she snatched Lieutenant Pluffles ("The Rescue of Pluffles") from the vampire hold of Mrs. Reiver, the woman about whom there was "nothing good unless it was her dress." This, by the way,

Photograph by Brown Bros.

JAKKO HILL: "DEODAR-CROWNED JAKKO," THE HIGHEST OF THE SIMLA HILLS

Princess, behold our ancient state
  Has clean departed, and we see
'Twas idleness we took for fate
  That bound light bonds on you and me.

Amen! here ends the comedy
  Where it began in all good will;
Since love and leave together flee
  As driven mist on Jakko hill!

—*A Ballade of Jakko Hill*

was the same Mrs. Reiver who figures in the story "In Error" (*Plain Tales from the Hills*) as the unconscious saviour of Moriarty.

Mrs. Hauksbee again came to the rescue of a misguided youth when she saved young Peythroppe of "Kidnapped" (*Plain Tales from the Hills*) from marriage with the "impossible" Miss Castries.

Leaving the Mall, you come to Jakko Hill, guarding the town on the East. It was near Jakko, just below the Town Hall, that Kim met the Hindu boy sent to guide him to the house of Lurgan Sahib:

> Together they set off through the mysterious dusk, full of the noises of a city below the hillside, and the breath of a cool wind in deodar-crowned Jakko, shouldering the stars. The house-lights, scattered on every level, made, as it were, a double firmament. Some were fixed, others belonged to the 'rickshaws of careless, open-spoken English folk, going out to dinner.

All Simla rides round Jakko Hill. "A Ballade of Jakko Hill" breathes of the spirit of social life at Simla as Kipling saw it:

> Woman, behold our ancient state
>   Has clean departed; and we see
> 'Twas Idleness we took for Fate
>   That bound light bonds on you and me.
> Amen! here ends the comedy
>   Where it began in all good will,
> Since Love and Leave together flee
>   As driven mist on Jakko Hill!

In their ride round Jakko Hill, the lovers in "The Hill of Illusion" (*Under the Deodars*) learned—fortunately not too late—that "the eternal constancy," "unalterable trust," "reverent devotion," and "honour" so often sworn toward each other, had not so solid a foundation as they had imagined when they planned their elopement at Shaifazehat a few months before; and they virtually withdrew from their compact while the echoes of Mrs. Buzgago's solo rang in their ears:

See saw! Margery Daw!
Sold her bed to lie upon straw.
Wasn't she a silly slut
To sell her bed and lie upon dirt?

Jakko comes into the visions of the man who, in "La Nuit Blanche," writes of his sensations during an attack of *delirium tremens:*

I had seen as dawn was breaking
  And I staggered to my rest,
Tara Devi softly shaking
  From the Cart Road to the crest.
I had seen the spurs of Jakko
  Heave and quiver, swell and sink;
Was it Earthquake or tobacco,
  Day of Doom or Night of Drink?

A favourite place for the appearance of the phantom 'rickshaw was the Jakko Road. Jack Pansay and

THE BROAD ROAD AROUND JAKKO HILL

All Simla rides around Jakko Hill. Here Jack Pansay was riding with Kitty Mannering when he saw again the Phantom 'Rickshaw. On the Jakko Road you again meet with Mrs. Hauksbee, and below the road lies the little English cemetery where the "Tertiam Quid" gazed down into the grave which was so soon to become his own, "nasty and cold—horribly cold"

Kitty Mannering were riding together round Jakko when, after Pansay's well-grounded hope of relief from "The Horror," he saw again the phantom 'rickshaw; dragged Kitty by the wrist up to where the phantom stood; revealed, in the insanity of his terror, the whole story of his relations with Mrs. Wessington; and received Kitty's dismissal in the lash of her riding-whip across his face. It was on the Jakko Road, too, that Pansay begged the ghost of Agnes Wessington to explain the meaning of her endless persecution of him, and there he had his answer.

On the Jakko Road, you again meet with Mrs. Hauksbee. It was while her 'rickshaw loitered round Jakko that Mrs. Hauksbee, in "The Education of Otis Yeere," preached to Otis Yeere the Great Gospel of Conceit; and unconsciously taught him more than conceit; for through his dreams "ran, as sheet-lightning through golden cloud, the light of Mrs. Hauksbee's violet eyes." Mrs. Hauksbee was riding round Jakko with "the Hawley Boy," when they met the "Dancing Master," and the "Dowd," whose unkempt appearance inspired Mrs. Hauksbee, when next she saw her bosom friend, Mrs. Mallowe, to a vast amount of scornful wit. The Jakko Road also knew well "The Man's Wife" and the "Tertiam Quid" ("At the Pit's Mouth"); and Jakko Road overlooks the little English cemetery where the "Tertiam Quid" gazed down into the grave which was so soon to become his own, "nasty and cold—horribly cold." This cemetery is the "cool rest-house down the glen," of "Possibilities,"

His place forgets him; other men
  Have bought his ponies, guns, and traps.
  His fortune is the Great Perhaps
And that cool rest-house down the glen,

Whence he shall hear, as spirits may,
  Our mundane revel on the height,
  Shall watch each flashing *'rickshaw*-light
Sweep on to dinner, dance, and play.

"A Ballad of Burial" tells of a plainsman's longing to be carried after death to that little cemetery at Simla:

I could never stand the Plains.
  Think of blazing June and May,
Think of those September rains
  Yearly till the Judgment Day!
I should never rest in peace,
  I should sweat and lie awake.
Rail me then, on my decease,
  To the Hills for old sake's sake.

The cemetery is mentioned again in "An Old Song" as "those grim glades below,"

Where heedless of the flying hoof
  And clamour overhead,
Sleep, with the grey langur for guard
  Our very scornful Dead.

Copyright by Underwood & Underwood, N. Y.

SIMLA—THE LOWER BAZAAR

The Simla home of Mahbub Ali (*Kim*) ". . . the crowded rabbit-warren that climbs up to the Town Hall at an angle of forty-five. A man who knows his way there can defy all the police of India's summer capital, so cunningly does veranda communicate with veranda, alley-way with alley-way, and bolt-hole with bolt-hole. Here live grocers, oil-sellers, curio-venders, fire-wood dealers, priests, pickpockets, and native employees of the Government; here are discussed by courtesans all the things which are supposed to be profoundest secrets of the India Council; and here gather all the sub-sub-agents of half the native States"

The Himalayan-Thibet Road, which leads off from the Jakko Road

is no more than six feet wide in most places, and the drop into the valley below may be anything between one and two thousand feet.

It was along this path that the "Tertiam Quid" rode to his ghastly fate.

In Chota Simla, only a short distance from the cemetery, is "Benmore," once a ballroom, now a Government office, and loved by all longtime residents of Simla for old sake's sake. "The Lover's Litany" is a witness to this affection:

Eyes of blue—the Simla Hills
Silvered with the moonlight hoar;
Pleading of the waltz that thrills,
Dies and echoes round Benmore.
"*Mabel*," "*Officers*," "*Good-bye*,"
Glamour, wine, and witchery—
On my soul's sincerity,
"*Love like ours can never die!*"

"The Plea of the Simla Dancers" expresses their plaintive indignation when Benmore was changed from a ballroom into a Government office:

Too late, alas! the song
To remedy the wrong;—
The rooms are taken from us, swept and garnished for their fate,
But these tear-besprinkled pages
Shall attest to future ages
That we cried against the crime of it—too late, alas! too late!

And regarding the dead comrade in "Possibilities," we read,

> Benmore shall woo him to the ball
> With lighted rooms and braying band;
> And he shall hear and understand
> "*Dream Faces*" better than us all.

Miss Hollis of the "big, quiet, grey eyes," suddenly released from the spell of the "Bisara of Pooree" learned at Benmore her terrible mistake and withdrew from her engagement to Pack. Benmore was still a ballroom when Strickland ("Miss Youghal's *Sais*") used to wait outside for Miss Youghal:

> Strickland's account of the agony he endured on wet nights, hearing the music and seeing the lights in "Benmore," with his toes tingling for a waltz and his head in a horse-blanket, is rather amusing.

Climbing steeply downward below Jakko, you come to the lower bazar, the Simla home of Mahbub Ali (*Kim*),

> the crowded rabbit-warren that climbs up from the valley to the Town Hall at an angle of forty-five. A man who knows his way there can defy all the police of India's summer capital, so cunningly does verandah communicate with verandah, alley-way with alley-way, and bolt-hole with bolt-hole. Here live those who minister to the wants of the city—*jhampanis* who pull the pretty ladies' 'rick-

shaws by night and gamble till the dawn, grocers, oil-sellers, curio-vendors, fire-wood dealers, priests, pickpockets, and native employees of the Government; here are discussed by courtesans all the things which are supposed to be profoundest secrets of the India Council; and here gather all the sub-sub-agents of half the native States.

III
THE HIMALAYAS

III

The Himalayas

FOLLOWING the Himalayan-Thibet Road from Simla, the traveller comes to the higher Himalayas, one of the most delightful regions on the face of the globe. Warm green valleys, all sunshine and soft air and flowers and bird songs, sweep upward with astounding abruptness to great forests of pines and deodars swathed in moss and fern where cloud wreaths chase each other in the high wind and the edelweiss hides among the rocks; and up and up to giant glaciers and ice-bound peaks that pierce the very sky. Once enthralled by the spirit of the Himalaya Mountains you will hardly escape, for it is the spirit of enormous distances, tremendous heights, and terrific depths; the spirit of loud laughter of mountain torrent and the solemn stillness of densest woodland, of damp earth smells, of black, impenetrable shadow and blazing, blinding light; the spirit of glorious colour on plant and bird and beast, on rock and cloud and snow.

Small wonder that Captain Gadsby and his bride ("The Garden of Eden"), spending their honeymoon in the Himalayas near the Fagoo Hills, thought themselves in the Garden of Eden, and that they had "appropriated all the happiness in the world!" The Himalayas saw another interview between Captain Gadsby and a lady when there was not so much happiness abroad. Naini Tal in the Himalayas, a charming little summer resort, was the place where Captain Gadsby, during an agonizing dinner hour, "explained things" to the incomparable "Harriet Herriott" ("The Tents of Kedar").

"Far and far in the Hills" Kim and his mild old lama and Hurree Babu adventured, the lama always longing for higher and yet higher hills. "Oh! the hills, and the snow upon the hills!" was his yearning cry while the plainsmen tried in vain to keep pace with him as "with steady, driving strokes from the loins he strode upwards." "Shamlegh" is one of the many Himalaya Mountain villages of rude little huts "perched on the edge of all things," where the trees are filled with fluttering bits of paper bearing the inscription, written over and over again, "*Om mani padme, om!*" (Hail to the Holy One [Buddha] whose jewel is the lotus, hail!) It was here that the

> "woman of Shamlegh" (*Kim*) "a fair-coloured woman . . . aught but unlovely . . . with turquoise-studded headgear,"

so hospitably entertained Kim and the lama. "Shamlegh" is not far from Kotgarh, where there is a little colony of English people, an English mission, and a tel-

"Tibetan Devil-dance masks . . . horned masks, scowling masks, and masks of idiotic terror"—*Kim*

"Oh, the hills and the snow upon the hills!"—*Kim*

LAHORE
—An old Gate

Through this gate in the "wonderful walled city of Lahore" Kim and the Lama passed on their search for the River of the Arrow and the Red Bull on a Green Field—*Kim*

egraph station. Perhaps the woman of Shamlegh was "Lispeth" (*Plain Tales from the Hills*), the Christian girl of the Kotgarh Mission who was "beautiful, like the Princesses in fairy tales," and who returned to her own people because an English *Sahib* had betrayed her trust.

Just out of Kotgarh is "the pass called Muttianee" ("The Truce of the Bear") through which "Matun, the old blind beggar" went down to hunt the bear and just beyond which he responded so disastrously to the truce of the bear. Chini is not far from Kotgarh. Dumoise, the Civil Surgeon of Meridki in the Punjab ("By Word of Mouth"), after the death of his wife and just before he died of cholera at Nuddea in Bengal, went on a walking tour to Chini.

——and the scenery is good if you are in trouble. You pass through big, still deodar-forests, and under big, still cliffs, and over big, still grass-downs swelling like a woman's breasts; and the wind across the grass and the rain among the deodars say—'Hush—hush—hush!'

Just beyond, in Bagi, a cold, lonely little Hill station, Ram Dass, the bearer, saw the dead Mrs. Dumoise

'walking on the road to the village. She was in a blue dress, and she lifted the veil of her bonnet and said—"Ram Dass, give my *salaams* to the *Sahib*, and tell him that I shall meet him next month at Nuddea."'

At a village of the Himalayas near Donga Pa—the Mountain of the Council of the Gods—Athira, wife of

Madu, the charcoal-burner, "one-eyed and of a malignant disposition," and Suket Singh, Sepoy of the 102d Punjab Native Infantry ("Through the Fire") learned to love each other "better than life," and because of an evil fate forbidding that love, they chose death by their own hands rather than separation. The men of Donga Pa across the valley saw

> a great fire . . . winking and blazing through the night, and said that the charcoal-burners of Kodru were getting drunk. But it was only Suket Singh . . . and Athira . . . burning—burning—burning.

"On the road to Thibet, very many miles in the Himalayas," lay a certain kingdom,

> eleven thousand feet above the sea and exactly four miles square; but most of the miles stood on end owing to the nature of the country.

There, "between the tail of a heaven-climbing glacier and a dark birch-forest" was the hut of "Namgay Doola" (*Life's Handicap*) "whom his fellow-villagers called the outlander," because of his flaming red hair and his merry blue eyes, and because he worshipped the strange God of the Crucifix. And Namgay Doola drove to despair his gentle-hearted King, whose revenues "were rather less than four hundred pounds yearly," and whose standing army consisted of five men armed with utterly useless implements of war. Nam-

MOUNT KINCHINJUNGA
"The Eternal Snow" of the Himalayas

"A HEAVEN-CLIMBING GLACIER"

"The true hills," the goal of the Lama's pilgrimage with Kim. "Above them, changeless since the world's beginning, but changing to every mood of sun and cloud, lay out the eternal snow"—*Kim*

gay Doola was the King's most expert log snatcher when the great deodar logs became jammed in the stream; and he was "a man of a merry face"; but he refused to pay revenue, stirred up treason among his fellows, and committed "sacrilege unspeakable against the Holy Cow," until the King's English guest, who understood Namgay Doola and his race, solved the problem and set the matter straight. He listened to Namgay Doola's queer Lepcha version of "The Wearing of the Green,"

> 'Dir hané mard-i-yemen dir
> To weeree ala gee.'
> (They're hanging men and women, too,
> For the wearing of the green);

learned that Namgay Doola was the son of Tim Doolan, an Irish soldier in an East India regiment, and knew that Namgay Doola's acts were prompted by the hereditary instincts of that

> "quaint, crooked, sweet, profoundly irresponsible and profoundly lovable race that fight like fiends, argue like children, obey like men, and jest like their own goblins of the rath through rebellion, want, woe, or war."

Wherefore, the King, on the advice of his friend, raised Namgay Doola, the rebel, to the position of Commander-in-Chief of the Army

> "with honour . . . and full allowance of work . . . and liquor from certain bottles"

but not "a tuft of grass for his own."

IV
THE GREAT DESERT

IV

The Great Desert

MAKING his way back through Simla and down to the Plains, the traveller turns southward, and journeying now by metre gauge and now by the broad, regular line of the Indian Railway, finds himself after a few hours in the heart of the Rajputana Desert, with all its solemn grandeur and all its bitter desolation. Miles and miles of yellow sand stretch away to the horizon, broken only by great boulders, ragged camel's-thorn bushes, and little scrubby trees, or, perhaps, a whirling dust cloud, which rises high in air, scatters, and settles again. Here and there the waters of a lake or river, blue and sparkling in the blazing sunshine, refresh the eye; or low hills, purple in the distance, grow larger, clearer, and less fascinating as one nears their bare, brown ridges destitute of verdure. Again, thatch-roofed native huts peep out from flaunting, bright-coloured foliage in a great patch of forest land where, among the rocks and trees, tigers and leopards and wolves abound. As everywhere else in India, monkeys romp and chatter among the trees, little striped squirrels dart into sight and off again, and the green parrot looks down critically from a distant bough. Occasionally, a solitary camel, the jaws and brow of its rider bound tightly against the dust, weaves across the plain; a country bullock-cart creaks dismally along with its burden of men or cotton; or a band of gypsies, with wild, dark eyes, splendid bodies, and rainbow attire, pass slowly by, driving their cattle, the ornaments of the women, bone and iron and brass, clanking loudly. The heat is tremendous, and one wilts visibly in mind and body and apparel; the blazing sunshine blinds the eyes, and one is glad indeed when the waning light brings relief and the much-vaunted colouring of the desert—amber, gold, opal, green, and crimson—spreads over the landscape. This is the country

——where the wild dacoits abound
  And the Thakurs live in castles on the hills,
Where the *bunnia* and *bunjara* in alternate streaks are found,
  And the Rajah cannot liquidate his bills.

The trackless desert of Upper Rajputana, far from the railway line, was the scene of "The Strange Ride of Morrowbie Jukes" (*Under the Deodars*), the Civil Engineer who, in the delirium of fever, rode madly over the sandy plain, brandishing his hog spear at the moon and shouting challenges at the camel's-thorn bushes, and plunged without warning into the terrible village in-

Photograph by Brown Bros., N. Y.

CHINI IN THE HIMALAYAS

"You pass through big, still, deodar-forests, and under big, still cliffs, and over big, still grass-downs swelling like a woman's breasts; and the wind across the grass and the rain among the deodars say—'Hush—hush—hush'"—*By Word of Mouth*

habited by "the Dead who did not die but may not live."

The events told of in "At the End of the Passage" (*Life's Handicap*) probably took place also in this desert country. Hummil, the Assistant Engineer, and his three friends, who had ridden so far for the sake of seeing a white man's face—"they were lonely folk who understood the dread meaning of loneliness"—spent doleful hours together in the terrific heat of an Indian summer on the plains—

The sky is lead and our faces are red,
  And the gates of Hell are opened and riven,
And the winds of Hell are loosened and driven,
And the dust flies up in the face of Heaven,
  And the clouds come down in a fiery sheet,
Heavy to raise and hard to be borne.
  And the soul of man is turned from his meat,
Turned from the trifles for which he has striven
  Sick in his body and heavy-hearted,
  And his soul flies up like the dust in the sheet
  Breaks from his flesh and is gone and departed,
As the blasts they blow on the cholera-horn.

And poor Hummil, maddened by the heat and loneliness, became the victim of "terror beyond the expression of any pen"—hunted to death by the "blind face that cries and can't wipe its eyes."

In an insignificant little town of Eastern Rajputana the policeman of "At Howli Thana" (*In Black and*

White), concocted that marvellous story of the Dacoity, which should save them from deserved punishment, and which failed so completely before the smile and the "many eyes" of Yunkum Sahib, the Assistant Commissioner, "Tiger of Gokral-Seetarun."

"Gokral-Seetarun" was the province where Nick Tarvin of Topaz, Colorado (*The Naulahka*), a gallant nineteenth-century knight, championed so loyally and successfully his lady-love and the pathetic little Maharaj Kunwar in the midst of the intrigues of a gypsy queen; and learned the invaluable lesson that

——it is not good for the Christian's health to hustle the Aryan brown,
For the Christian riles and the Aryan smiles and he weareth the Christian down;
And the end of the fight is a tombstone white with the name of the late deceased,
And the epitaph drear: "A fool lies here who tried to hustle the East."

Chitor (Gunnaur) is the Dead City where, in the "Gye-Mukh" or "Cow's Mouth" Nick sought the Naulahka, the priceless necklace of crown jewels which he afterward saw during the wedding pageant of the Maharaj Kunwar.

It blazed with the dull red of the ruby, the angry green of the emerald, the cold blue of the sapphire, and the white, hot glory of the diamond. But, dulling all these glories, was the superb radi-

THE LAND OF NAMGAY DOOLA

"On the road to Thibet, very many miles in the Himalayas," lay a certain Kingdom, "eleven thousand feet above the sea and exactly four miles square; but most of the miles stood on end owing to the nature of the country." There "between the tail of a heaven-climbing glacier and a dark birch-forest" was the hut of "Namgay Doola." (*Life's Handicap.*) It was here that the Special Correspondent found the Rajah with his standing army of four men, the red-headed Rebel with his red-headed Brood, and listened, puzzled, to the strange chant which had such a familiar ring

ance of one gem that lay above the great carved emerald on the central clasp. It was the black diamond—black as the pitch of the infernal lake, and lighted from below with the fires of Hell.

The thing lay on the boy's shoulders, a yoke of flame. It outshone the silent Indian stars above, turned the tossing torches to smears of dull yellow, and sucked the glitter from the cloth of gold on which it lay.

Chitor is on the railway line from Ajmir to Mhow. It was once the glorious capital of the Kings of Mewar and for hundreds of years was the scene of some of the greatest dramas in Indian history. At the beginning of the fourteenth century, Ala-ud-din Khilji, the Pathan emperor, having determined to capture the Rajput queen, Padmini, said to have been the most beautiful woman India has ever known, besieged the city of Chitor. When the Rajputs could no longer hold the place, all the thousands of women of the city, among them Queen Padmini, voluntarily went to their death on funeral pyres in the subterranean chambers of the palace, while the men dashed out of the gates into the very arms of their enemies, who entered the city over their dead bodies. Again Chitor came into the hands of the Rajputs and was not finally deserted until 1568, when Akbar besieged the place and the Maharana Udai Singh, considering the defence hopeless, left the city to its fate and betook himself some miles to the southwestward, where he founded the present city of Udaipur. Chitor is of remarkable shape and situation. Three miles in length, it stands on the summit of a huge rock five hundred feet above the plain, the massive loop-holed walls giving the city the appearance of a great battleship. New Chitor, a comparatively modern town of grain merchants and armourers, nestles at the base of the fortress, but within the old city there is no sign of human life. The beautiful palace of Padmini, the fine old temples, the big empty reservoirs, and wind-swept houses are given over to the birds and beasts of the jungle. The trees and the elements have torn great rents in the walls and many of the houses and tombs are ruined. In the midst of this ancient grandeur stands the old Jain Tower of Victory, one hundred and fifty feet high. In the side of a huge pit close by and reached from above by a flight of old stone steps is the Gye-Mukh, a sacred shrine surrounded by trees and ruined tombs and ornamented with heroic stone figures of gods carved in high relief. The Gye-Mukh takes its name from springs issuing from the sides of the pit through crude cow-mouth carvings, and falling into a reservoir filled with slimy purple water. From the Gye-Mukh, a passage leads into the subterranean chambers of Padmini's palace, where the queen and her loyal women went to their death. It was in this passage that Nick Tarvin's foot crashed into a skull and he retreated from the gruesome heaps of human bones and the wild emerald-eyed guardian of the place.

Rajputana contains some of the most conservative, fanatical Hindus of India. It was in Rajputana that

THE RAJPUTANA DESERT

This desert is a factor in numerous Kipling tales. It was the scene of "the strange ride of Morrowbie Jukes," the civil engineer who, in his fever, rode into the terrible village inhabited by "the dead who did not die but may not live." It is associated with the events related in *At the End of the Passage*. It plays a conspicuous part in *The Naulahka*. It knew Carnehan and Dravot of *The Man Who Would Be King*. It is the country

"—where the wild dacoits abound
and the Thakurs live in castles on the hills,
where the "Bunnia" and "Bunjara" in alternate streaks are found
and the Rajah cannot liquidate his bills."

infanticide was practised to the greatest extent, and it was here that the custom of suttee, the burning of the living widow on the pyre of her dead husband, survived longest. In Western Rajputana "The Last Suttee" took place; when, as the dead Rajput King lay on his funeral pyre and

> ——the death-fire leaped
> From ridge to river-head,
> From the Malwa plains to the Abu scaurs:

the Queen, disguised as a dancing girl, escaped from the palace, and fearing the flames but longing to share the death of her lord, besought the baron guarding the pyre to kill her and burn her with the king.

> He drew and struck: the straight blade drank
> The life beneath the breast.
> 'I had looked for the Queen to face the flame,
> 'But the harlot dies for the Rajpoot dame—
> 'Sister of mine, pass, free from shame.
> 'Pass with thy King to rest!'
>
> The black log crashed above the white:
> The little flames and lean,
> Red as slaughter and blue as steel,
> That whistled and fluttered from head to heel,
> Leaped up anew, for they found their meal
> On the heart of—the Boondi Queen!

It was near here, in Pali, that the twins of "Gemini" (*In Black and White*) were born, the money-lenders of

Isser Jang, whom Durga Dass, one of the twins, described so accurately when he portrayed his brother:

——a swine and a night-thief, a taker of life, an eater of flies, a jackal-spawn without beauty, or faith, or cleanliness, or honour.

Here in Western Rajputana, we come on the trail of Peachey Carnehan and Daniel Dravot of "The Man Who Would Be King" (*Under the Deodars*). Nasirabad is an unimportant little town on the metre gauge line of railway running from Ajmir to Mhow; and it was here that the Special Correspondent made the acquaintance of Carnehan.

a big, black-browed gentleman in shirt-sleeves,—a wanderer and a vagabond,—but with an educated taste for whiskey."

who

told tales of things he had seen and done, of out-of-the-way corners of the Empire into which he had penetrated, and of adventures in which he risked his life for a few days' food.

and who finally sent a message by the Correspondent to his friend Dravot at Marwar Junction. Just to the west, on the railway line of the Bombay Mail, lies Marwar Junction, another town of no special importance, where in the second-class railway carriage the Cor-

ELEPHANT CAPARISONED FOR A STATE PAGEANT

The elephants in the wedding pageant of the Maharaj Kunwar were decked out in this fashion
—*The Naulahka*

respondent obligingly sought out Dravot, the man with "a flaming red beard" and "a great and shining face," and gave him the mysterious message, "He has gone South for the week." Following close after the clever adventurers, you find them in some large city of the Punjab, probably Lahore, seeking in the hot newspaper office of the friendly Correspondent information concerning Kafiristan which, with consummate impudence and boundless ambition, they have decided to conquer and rule as kings, according to their "Contrack" with each other:

> This Contract between me and you persuing witnesseth in the name of God—Amen and so forth.
>
> (One) That me and you will settle this matter together; i. e., to be Kings of Kafiristan.
>
> (Two) That you and me will not, while this matter is being settled, look at any Liquor, nor any Woman black, white, or brown, so as to get mixed up with one or the other harmful.
>
> (Three) That we conduct ourselves with Dignity and Discretion, and if one of us gets into trouble the other will stay by him.
>
> Signed by you and me this day.
>
> Peachey Taliaferro Carnehan.
> Daniel Dravot.
> Both Gentlemen at Large.

Then comes the departure from the Serai (probably the Kashmir Serai of Lahore), Dravot disguised as a mad native priest and Carnehan as his servant, travelling on camels ostensibly to "the North to sell charms that are never still to the Amir," but carrying, concealed beneath the camel-bags, twenty Martinis and "ammunition to correspond."

V

THE BORDER COUNTRY

V

The Border Country

PESHAWUR, a mud-walled town with houses of mud and rough bricks, is a large British military station only a few miles from the Afghan frontier. Here Carnehan and Dravot joined the caravan of the trader going through the Khyber Pass to Kabul, the capital of Afghanistan.

For more than six hundred miles, India is bordered on the northwest by Afghanistan, the savage country of a savage race—large, muscular, war-like Mahomedans—often called "Pathans"—unruly and fanatical—which, ever since the early nineteenth century, has been at war, more or less constant, with British India. No European is allowed to live in the country—which is made to act as a "buffer" state between Russia and India—the Amir, as the ruler of Afghanistan is called, being guided in all foreign affairs by the Indian Government, from which he receives an annual subsidy.

Afghanistan is a country of violent contrasts. Day after day the traveller fights his way through the rough narrow defiles of lofty, jagged mountains, cold and bleak and desolate, or over sandy, fever-stricken deserts, suddenly to find himself in the midst of a pleasant summer valley whose fertile orchards and vineyards produce some of the finest fruits in the world. Ten miles west of Peshawur, in a group of marvellous caves, begins the Khyber Pass, "that narrow sword-cut in the hills," which runs back fifty miles to the centre of Afghanistan. This famous mountain pass, which sometimes narrows to the bed of a tiny rivulet, the cliffs on each side rising almost perpendicularly to the height of six or seven hundred feet, is the highway for the caravans coming from Central Asia into India.

Along this mountain pass, Carnehan and Dravot made their way with the Afghan traders, the amusing antics of Dravot, "the mad priest," making him a welcome guest among the friendly natives. Leaving the caravans just below Jagdallak, a little mountain town between Peshawur and Kabul, they made their toilsome way through the mountains, "tall and black" and "bitter cold, . . . with never a road broader than the back of your hand," past hostile villages, "dispersed and solitary," and so to Kafiristan.

Kafiristan, a small tract of land in the northeastern part of Afghanistan, is but little known to the civilized world, whose only source of information is the account of the Mahomedan traders who have entered the country. From these it has been learned that Kafiristan, whose mountains are the higher peaks of the

THE TOWER OF VICTORY, CHITOR
"—the City of the Dead."

"Tall-built, sharp-domed palaces . . . revealed the horror of their emptiness and glared at the day that pierced them through and through. The wind passed singing down the empty streets, and, finding none to answer, returned, chasing before it a muttering cloud of dust, which presently whirled itself into a little cyclone funnel, and laid down with a sigh. . . . Gigantic reservoirs dry and neglected . . . hollow guard-houses that studded the battlements . . . time-riven arches that spanned the streets, and, above all, the carven tower with a shattered roof that sprang a hundred and fifty feet into the air, for a sign to the countryside that the royal city . . . was not dead, but would one day hum with men"—*The Naulahka*

Hindu Kush, is a far more attractive country than the rest of Afghanistan. The hillsides, thickly wooded with oak and pine, and the green valleys, rich in gardens and orchards and rolling meadows, resemble the Himalayan country, while the people, a pure type of Aryans, are remarkable for strength and beauty, many of the Kafirs—in strange contrast with their neighbours on every side—being as fair as Europeans, with yellow hair, blue eyes, and pink cheeks. The women especially are said to be the handsomest women of the Orient. The Kafirs ("Kafiristan" meaning "the country of unbelievers in Islam") have resisted all attempts to convert them to the Moslem faith, clinging tenaciously to their ancient form of worship, which closely resembles the old Vedic religion. While the people are barbaric in many ways, using bows and arrows for weapons, and dressing chiefly in goat's skin and goat's hair, they sit on stools after the manner of Europeans and have several other European customs.

Into this country of Kafiristan Peachey and Dravot suddenly precipitated themselves before the simple natives, who received them as gods; here by masterly strategem they won their sovereignty; and here the tragic farce ended with the murder of Dravot, hurled to death from the rope bridge, and the journey of Peachey, hopelessly maimed and mad and bearing with him the crowned head of Dravot, back to the hot newspaper office in India to tell his piteous tale.

Through the cruel border country, Lieutenant Austin

Limmason of the White Hussars ("The Man Who Was") in his terrible flight from Siberia somehow fought through to Peshawur, until "like a homing pigeon he had found his way to his own old mess," who were entertaining royally but reluctantly Dirkovitch, the Russian; and proved his right to be there by his mechanical, accurate response to the "Queen's toast," that "Sacrament of the Mess" which "never grows old, and never ceases to bring a lump into the throat of the listener wherever he be by sea or land":

——the colonel rose, but his hand shook, and the port spilled on the table as he looked straight at the man . . . and said hoarsely, "Mr. Vice, the Queen." There was a little pause, but the man sprung to his feet and answered without hesitation, "The Queen, God bless her!" and as he emptied the thin glass he snapped the shank between his fingers.

Peshawur and the Border saw the mutiny of the Native Irregular Cavalry ("The Lost Legion"), who were afterward hunted to their death by the Afghans while they rode

——stumbling and rocking in their saddles, and howling for mercy . . . from hill to hill, from ravine to ravine, up and down the dried beds of rivers and round the shoulders of bluffs, till it disappeared as water sinks in the sand—this officerless rebel regiment."

And all because the Pathans

"desired their clothes, and their bridles, and their rifles, and their boots,—and more especially their boots . . . a great killing —done slowly."

Copyright by Underwood & Underwood, N. Y.

THE KHYBER PASS

Below the famous fort of Ali Masjid, showing the Khyber rifles on the march. It was through this cruel border country that Austin Limmason of the White Hussars, *The Man Who Was*, forced his way in his terrible flight from Siberia. This is also the country of the battle described in *Drums of the Fore and Aft*, of *The Lost Legion*, of *Love o' Women*, of *Wee Willie Winkie*, and of *With the Main Guard*

And many years later, among the Border Hills, when the long-suffering British Government moved at last against the outlawed Gulla Kutta Mulla, the ghosts of the Lost Legion, stumbling about among their own graves, won an easy victory for the British.

Near the Edwardes Gate in Peshawur lived Suddhoo's son ("In the House of Suddhoo") whose attack of pleurisy indirectly cost his father so many rupees and brought upon his father's friends so much perturbation of spirit, all through the cunning machinations of the seal-cutter.

On the road to Peshawur, the sight of the simple, honest love between Mulvaney and his Dinah Shadd, with the "flower hand, foot av shod air, an' the eyes av the livin' mornin'," brought an agony of remorse and shame to "Love-o'-Women" (*Many Inventions*) of the Black Tyrone, a "gentleman-ranker" such as those who are told of in "Gentleman-Rankers."

We have done with Hope and Honour, we are lost to Love and
    Truth,
We are dropping down the ladder rung by rung,
And the measure of our torment is the measure of our youth.
God help us, for we knew the worst too young!
Our shame is clean repentance for the crime that brought the sen-
    tence,
Our pride it is to know no spur of pride,
And the Curse of Reuben holds us till an alien turf enfolds us
And we die, and none can tell Them where we died.
    We're poor little lambs who've lost our way,
        Baa! Baa! Baa!

We're little black sheep who've gone astray,
Baa—aa—aa!
Gentleman-rankers out on the spree,
Damned from here to Eternity,
God ha' mercy on such as we,
Baa! Yah! Bah!

And it was in Peshawur later on that same day that the death of "Love-o'-Women" and of his "Diamonds and Pearls" in each other's arms closed their tragic story—"a lamentable tale of things done long ago and ill done."

The tale of "Silver's Theatre," where "Love-o'-Women" tried so hard to die and failed, was told by Mulvaney ("With the Main Guard") to "blandandher" his suffering comrades through "a stifling June night" when "the heat under the bricked archway was terrifying," when "a puff of burning wind lashed through the wicket-gate like a wave of the sea," and "the dust-devils danced on the glacis and scoured the red-hot plain." "Silver's Theatre" was the name given by Mulvaney and his friends to "a gut betune two hills, as black as a bucket, an' as thin as a girl's waist," where the British and the Afghan soldiers

"just rushed into each other's arrums, an' there was no firing for a long time. Nothin' but knife an' bay'nit when we cud get our hands free: an' that was not often"—knee to knee—breast to breast—"breathin' in each other's faces and swearin' powerful."

ROPE BRIDGE OVER A MOUNTAIN TORRENT

It was such a bridge of "dizzy dancing ropes" that the Kafirs cut, sending Dravot to his death
—*The Man Who Would Be King*

Terence Mulvaney, John Learoyd, and Stanley Ortheris are described by their friend, the Special Correspondent, as

> three men who loved each other so greatly that neither man nor woman could come between them—in no sense refined, nor to be admitted to the outer-door mats of decent folk, because they happened to be private soldiers in her Majesty's army; and private soldiers . . . have small time for self-culture . . . their duty
>
> being
>
> to keep themselves and their accoutrements specklessly clean, to refrain from getting drunk more often than is necessary, to obey their superiors, and to pray for a war . . . the worst men in the regiment so far as genial blackguardism goes."

These "Three Musketeers" stood firm in the crush at "Silver's Theatre," Mulvaney with his "bay'nit, wid a long reach, a double twist—an' a slow recover," Learoyd with the rifle-butt "used exactly as a man would use a dagger," and little Ortheris with his "breech that's wore out a bit, an' amminition one year in store, to let the powder kiss the bullet"; while Captain O'Niel—the beloved "Cruikna-bulleen"—led his men on with a cheery laugh; while the Sergeant of the Tyrone sat on the head of the weeping and cursing "little orf'cer-bhoy" to save him alive for his mother in Ireland; and while the Black Tyrone fought "like sowls in tormint," for they had seen their dead mutilated with the soul-sickening mutilation that the Afghan women inflict on the dead and wounded of their enemy.

Ortheris had a still better chance to show his skill with the rifle when from a pine grove near the Border he shot the deserter of the Aurungabadis ("On Greenhow Hill") "seven hundred yards away and fully two hundred down the hillside." That was the afternoon that Learoyd, lying under the pines, tore up a handful of white violets and told the tale of his lost love, the girl of Greenhow Hill in England, to win whom he had nearly committed "black murder," and who, when he had enlisted in the army, gave him a last caress and whispered with dying lips, "Eh, but I'd a' liked to see thee i' thy red coat, John, for thou was allus my own lad—my very own lad, and none else."

Mulvaney, Learoyd, and Ortheris appear again in that Border tale where Lord Benira Trig ("The Three Musketeers") made himself obnoxious to the regiment by desiring the garrisons to be turned out for his inspection on a holiday when "he would . . . dine with the Officer Commanding, and insult him, across the Mess table, about the appearance of the troops." This was at "Helanthami Cantonment," on the frontier and the three friends devised a scheme, which proved most successful, to have Lord Benira "dacoited" by mischievous Buldoo and his friends, who were to pose as Pathans, and "gallantly rescued" by themselves—all that the objectionable earl might be made unfit to inspect troops until their holiday should be past.

Fort Pearson, near Kalabagh, is another frontier fort, and there took place the events told of by Crandall Minor, the young Subaltern (*Stalky & Co.*), as he lay in the darkness of the college dormitory and "spoke to the generation he could not see"—how Duncan of the old College, in command of a cartload of rupees to pay off the troops, was attacked by the Pathans, deserted by his Sepoy escort, and found by his schoolmate, Crandall, "under the wheels of the cart out in the open, propped up on one arm, blazing away with a revolver"; and how he died a few moments later with his head on his comrade's knees. In later years three or four of this "younger generation" bravely suppressed the Khye-Kheen-Malot uprising over the Border (*Stalky & Co.*) when "Stalky" showed the same remarkable ability as a strategist that had distinguished him in his boyhood days at college.

It was during a fierce fight on the frontier that Captain Gadsby of the Pink Hussars (*Story of the Gadsbys*) "led at Amdheran after Bagal-Deasin went under, and" they

> were all mixed up together; . . . . went through the guns . . . like a devil possessed of devils; . . . left his sword . . . In an Uttmanzai's head;

and "came out of the show dripping like a butcher." That was the day when Van Loo, Captain Gadsby's horse, fell on his rider's leg and an Afghan gave the Captain the ugly scar "all up the arm" which one memorable day roused Mrs. Gadsby's curiosity ("Fatima"). Then "Mafflin came round the corner and stopped the performance" by cutting off the Afghan's head. At night when the troops were picketed Gadsby promised Mafflin that he'd stick by him and the Pink Hussars as long as he lived ("The Swelling of Jordan"). This was the promise of which Mafflin mournfully reminded Gadsby when Gadsby told his old friend that he was going to leave the Service and go home to England for the sake of his wife and baby.

> White hands cling to the tightened rein,
>   Slipping the spur from the booted heel,
> Tenderest voices cry, "Turn again!"
>   Red lips tarnish the scabbarded steel,
> High hopes faint on a warm hearth-stone—
> He travels the fastest who travels alone.
>
> ("L'Envoi.")

It was Border warfare which showed Lieutenant George Cottar "The Brushwood Boy" (*The Day's Work*), "who bore with him from school and college a character worth much fine gold," how truly effective was the "machine of his love and labour"—his troop which he had guided with so much tact and skill.

> They were fit—physically fit beyond the other troops; they were good children in camp, wet or dry, fed or unfed; and they followed

AFGHANISTAN FROM THE KHYBER PASS

This is the entry into the country of the restless Afghans, the scene of many a border fight and raid in Kipling tales. Down through the Khyber Pass to Peshawur came our gruff and kindly friend Mahbub Ali with his caravan—*The Ballad of the King's Jest*

their officers with the quick suppleness and trained obedience of a first-class football fifteen.

But the honours won in that first campaign, his promotion, the Distinguished Service Order, and the idolatry of his regiment, did not prevent Major George Cottar—"the youngest major in the Army"—and whose ideals had kept him always from doing the "things no fellow can do"—from drifting back at night to the wonderful dreamland of his childhood, where the beautiful princess "Annie*an*louise" always played with him near the brushwood pile on the sandy beach.

A frontier scrimmage brought to an end "The Mutiny of the Mavericks" (*Life's Handicap*), the Irish Regiment which Mulcahy, the Irish-American, "devoured with blind, rancorous hatred of England," had tried with so much effort and beer to entangle in a conspiracy against the British Empire. On the field of "Marzun-Katai," Horse Egan and Dan Grady, "for the honour of the Regiment," urged the trembling, cowardly Mulcahy into the front ranks of the fight against the Afghans, until

the panic excess of his fear drove him into madness beyond all human courage. His eyes staring at nothing, his mouth open and frothing, and breathing as one in a cold bath, he went forward demented

to deeds of wild heroism; then "tore on, sobbing" and

alone into the midst of the retreating Afghans, until the "straight-held blade" of an Afghan "went home through the defenceless breast."

The 195th Regiment was stationed near the Border when "Wee Willie Winkie" (*Under the Deodars*), the Colonel's six-year-old son, saw Miss Allardyce cross the river into the dangerous Afghan territory, and promptly rode to the rescue, because Miss Allardyce belonged to his faithful friend and ally, "Coppy" (Lieutenant Brandis). The rescue was affected on the Afghan side of the Border when Wee Willie Winkie manfully faced the "Bad Men" until his regiment arrived, thus proving himself a "*pukka* hero" and winning the right to his own name, "Percival William Williams." Fort Jumrood on the Frontier is the background of that other story where a Colonel's son is a hero ("The Ballad of East and West") when Kamal, the Border chieftain, stole the Colonel's favourite mare and rode away. He was hotly pursued into his own territory beyond Jumrood by the Colonel's son, whose rash courage was so greatly admired by Kamal, that, although he held the boy's life at his mercy, he not only spared him, but took with him "the oath of Blood-Brother."

They have looked each other between the eyes, and there they
found no fault,
They have taken the Oath of the Brother-in-Blood on leavened
bread and salt;

JUMROOD AT SUNSET

Fort Jumrood is the background for *The Ballad of East and West*, when Kamal, the Border chieftain, stole the Colonel's favourite mare and was hotly pursued beyond Jumrood by the Colonel's son. *The Lament of the Border Cattle Thief* is also the tale of a Jumrood robber chief

They have taken the Oath of the Brother-in-Blood on fire and fresh-cut sod,
On the hilt and the haft of the Khyber knife, and the Wondrous Names of God.

. . . .

Oh, East is East, and West is West, and never the two shall meet,
Till Earth and Sky stand presently at God's great Judgment Seat;
But there is neither East nor West, Border, nor Breed, nor Birth,
When two strong men stand face to face, tho' they come from the ends of the earth.

"The Lament of the Border Cattle Thief" is also the tale of a Jumrood robber chief:

They have taken away my long jezail,
My shield and sabre fine,
And heaved me into the Central Jail
For lifting of the kine.

. . . . .

And God have mercy on the Jut
When once my fetters fall,
And Heaven defend the farmer's hut
When I am loosed from thrall.

. . . . .

Ride hard, ride hard to Abazai,
Young *Sahib* with the yellow hair—
Lie close, lie close as khuttucks lie,
Fat herds below Bonair!

The one I'll shoot at twilight tide,
  At dawn I'll drive the other;
The black shall mourn for hoof and hide,
  The white man for his brother!

This section of country appears again in "The Head of the District" (*Life's Handicap*). On the banks of the Indus River, near Peshawur, the dying Yardley-Orde, Deputy Commissioner of the "Kot-Kumharsen" District, bade good-bye to his friends and eagerly watched the approach of the boat carrying his wife, who arrived just one hour too late, "the grimmest practical joke ever played on a man." "Kot-Kumharsen," the district which was deprived of the wise and kind guidance of Yardley-Orde and left in the hands of a South-country Babu, lies under the Khusru Hills of the Frontier. Here it was that the Khusru Kheyl, urged on by the fiery eloquence of the Blind Mullah of Jagai, mutinied and made their unsuccessful attack on the low-land villages: while the South-country Babu, "born in a hothouse, of stock bred in a hothouse, and fearing physical pain as some men fear sin," fled in terror, and fever-stricken Tommy Dodd bade his fever-stricken men go forth, with the words,

"O men! If you die you will go to Hell. Therefore endeavour to keep alive. But if you go to Hell that place cannot be hotter than this place, and we are not told that we shall there suffer from fever. Consequently be not afraid of dying. File out there!"

And here Tallantire, the Assistant Deputy Commissioner, who knew "the talk and the heart of his people," ended his scathing denunciation of Khoda Dad Khan, chief of the mutinous tribes, with the words "Rest assured that the Government will send you a man"; and received from the Chief the praise he so richly deserved,

"Ay . . . for we also be men . . . And by God, Sahib may thou be that man!"

From the Hurrum Hills over the Border, Jones ("A Code of Morals") heliographed to his wife the love messages and warnings concerning her moral welfare, which were so inopportunely read off by General Bangs, riding with his Aide and Staff—

For clear as summer-lightning flare, the husband's warning ran:—
"Don't dance or ride with General Bangs—a most immoral man."

. . . .

All honour unto Bangs, for ne'er did Jones thereafter know
By word or act official who read off that helio.;
But the tale is on the Frontier, and from Michni to Mool*tan*
They know the worthy General as "that most immoral man."

Kurram Valley, referred to in "Arithmetic on the Frontier," is a beautiful bit of level, fertile country over the Border, whose inhabitants are among the wildest and most faithless of the Afghans.

A great and glorious thing it is
  To learn, for seven years or so,
The Lord knows what of that and this,
  Ere reckoned fit to face the foe—
The flying bullet down the Pass,
That whistles clear:—"All flesh is grass."

Three hundred pounds per annum spent
  On making brain and body meeter
For all the murderous intent
  Comprised in "villainous saltpetre!"
And after?—Ask the Yusufzaies
What comes of all our 'ologies.

. . . . . .

One sword-knot stolen from the camp
  Will pay for all the school expenses
Of any Kurram Valley scamp
  Who knows no word of moods and tenses,
But, being blest with perfect sight,
Picks off our messmates left and right.

By their pitiful retreat during a battle with the Afghans on the Frontier, "The Fore and Fit Princess Hohenzollern-Sigmaringen-Anspach's Merther-Tydfilshire Own Royal Loyal Light Infantry, Regimental District 329A" earned the title of "The Fore and Aft" ("The Drums of the Fore and Aft"), and were saved from everlasting disgrace by little Jakin and Lew, the twelve-year-old drummer boys who, all alone on the great plain strewn with the dead and wounded, marched stiffly with fife and drum into the face of the foe, calling

THE HINDU KUSH MOUNTAINS, NEAR QUETTA

"Jack Barrett's bones at Quetta enjoy profound repose" while his wife who remained behind at Simla "on three-fourths his monthly screw" "mourned for him five lively months at most"—*The Story of Uriah*

on their panic-stricken regiment to return and meet the enemy.

"And in bitter mockery of the distant mob, the old tune of the Old Line shrilled and rattled:

'But of all the world's great heroes
There's none that can compare,
With a tow—row—row—row—row—row,
To the British Grenadier!'"

And the sullen regiment responded with terrible disaster to the Afghans.

But some say, . . . that that battle was won by Jakin and Lew, whose little bodies were borne up just in time to fit two gaps at the head of the big ditch-grave for the dead under the heights of Jagai.

Down through the Khyber Pass to Peshawur came our gruff and kindly friend, Mahbub Ali ("The Ballad of the King's Jest"), with his caravan.

Lean are the camels but fat the frails,
Light are the purses but heavy the bales,
As the snowbound trade of the North comes down
To the market-square of Peshawur town.
In a turquoise twilight, crisp and chill,
A kafila camped at the foot of the hill.
Then blue smoke-haze of the cooking rose,
And tent-peg answered to hammer-nose,
And the picketed ponies shag and wild,

Strained at their ropes as the feed was piled;
And the bubbling camels beside the load
Sprawled for a furlong adown the road;
And the Persian pussy-cats brought for sale,
Spat at the dogs from the camel-bale;
And the tribesmen bellowed to hasten the food;
And the camp-fires twinkled by Fort Jumrood;
And there fled on the wings of the gathering dusk
A savour of camels and carpets and musk,
A murmur of voices, a reek of smoke,
To tell us the trade of the Khyber woke.

And there Mahbub Ali told his friend of the King's "jest," how the young lad, Wali Dad, sought favour at court by reporting as a fact that which was but a vague rumour, the coming of the Russians, and of how Abd-ur-Rahman, the Amir, determined to crush forever such empty reports, commanded the young man to sit in a peach tree overlooking the road to Kabul, and there to remain until the Russians should actually come.

"'Watch from the tree. Thou art young and strong,
Surely thy vigil is not for long.

. . . . .

Wait and watch. When the host is near
Shout aloud that my men may hear."

. . . . .

'A guard was set that he might not flee—
A score of bayonets ringed the tree.
The peach-bloom fell in showers of snow,
When he shook at his death as he looked below.
By the power of God, who alone is great,

THE INDUS RIVER, NEAR QUETTA

"Jack Barrett's bones at Quetta
Enjoy profound repose;
But I shouldn't be astonished
If now his spirit knows
The reason of his transfer
From the Himalayan snows."
—*The Story of Uriah*

Till the seventh day he fought with his fate.
Then madness took him, and men declare
He mowed in the branches as ape and bear,
And last as a sloth, ere his body failed,
And he hung as a bat in the forks, and wailed,
And sleep the cord of his hands untied,
And he fell, and was caught on the points and died.

"Ford o' Kabul River" is a ballad of the Border.

Ford, ford, ford o' Kabul River,
  Ford o' Kabul River in the dark!
Gawd 'elp 'em if they blunder, for their boots'll pull 'em under,
  By the ford o' Kabul River in the dark.

The tragedy of the man from Little Malikand ("Dray Wara Yow Dee") who, because she confessed her love for his rival, killed his young wife, formerly a maid of the Abazai, took place across the Border near Peshawur. From Little Malikand, the dishonoured husband, his "heart dried up with sorrow and shame,'" began his search for the author of his misery.

"and the head of the woman of the Abazai was before me night and day, even as it had fallen between my feet! . . . *Dray wara yow dee! Dray wara yow dee!* The body without the head, the soul without light, and my own darkling heart—all three are one—all three are one! . . . If my vengeance failed, I would splinter the gates of Paradise with the butt of my gun, or I would cut my way into Hell with my knife, and I would call upon Those who Govern there for the body of Daoud Shah. What love so deep as hate? . . . *Ahi! Ahi! Alghias! Ahi!*"

Journeying southward along the Border, the traveller comes to the important frontier station of Quetta in the Assigned British District of Baluchistan, and situated five thousand feet above sea level. Quetta was where Jack Barrett in "The Story of Uriah," was sent while his wife remained at Simla "on three-fourths his monthly screw"; and when Barret died "ere the next month's pay he drew," "mourned for him five lively months at most."

Jack Barrett's bones at Quetta
  Enjoy profound repose;
But I shouldn't be astonished
  If now his spirit knows
The reason of his transfer
  From the Himalayan snows.

And, when the Last Great Bugle Call
  Adown the Hurnai throbs,
When the last grim joke is entered
  In the big, black Book of Jobs,
And Quetta graveyards give again
  Their victims to the air,
I shouldn't like to be the man,
  Who sent Jack Barrett there.

The Quetta of to-day is a very different place, however, from the Quetta of the time of Jack Barrett. From a mudwalled cantonment, wretchedly lonely and unhealthful, it has grown to a prosperous, beautiful city of some twenty-five thousand inhabitants. Quetta, lying as it does in the path which a Russian invasion of India would probably take, is the most strongly fortified outpost of the British Empire in India. Although cruelly bleak and cold in the winter time, it has been, since the extension of its railway lines, one of the popular summer resorts of the north.

Southeast of Quetta, near Chachuran, is "Arti-goth" ("The Bubbling Well Road"), where grew the

> "patch of the plumed jungle-grass, that turns over in silver when the wind blows, from ten to twenty feet high and from three to four miles square,"

in which the hunter of pig and Mr. Wardle, his terrier, becoming lost, stumbled on the horrid mystery of the Bubbling Well and the evil priest of the Arti-goth "whose most pressing need" was "a halter and the care of the British Government."

VI

THE OLDEST LAND

VI

The Oldest Land

AND now we come back to the "Oldest Land":

> A stone's throw out on either hand
> From that well-ordered road we tread,
> And all the world is wild and strange:
> *Churel* and ghoul and *Djinn* and sprite
> Shall bear us company to-night,
> For we have reached the Oldest Land
> Wherein the Powers of Darkness range.
> (*From The Dusk to the Dawn.*)

From Peshawur on the northern boundary of India to Calcutta on the eastern boundary, is a journey of nearly two thousand miles. All along the way at frequent intervals crops out the Kipling country. A few generations ago, when India lacked her present-day railway facilities, the traveller would have taken his way by mail tonga or bullock-cart along the Grand Trunk Road which runs straight through from Peshawur to Calcutta. The Grand Trunk Road was the "broad road" spoken of by the Ressaldar when he guided Kim and the lama on their pilgrimage toward the south.

And now we come to the broad road . . —the great road which is the backbone of all Hind. For the most part it is shaded . . . with four lines of trees; the middle road—all hard—takes the quick traffic. In the days before rail-carriages the Sahibs travelled up and down here in hundreds. Now there are only country-carts and such like. Left and right is the rougher road for the heavy carts—grain and cotton and timber, bhoosa, lime, and hides. A man goes in safety here—for at every few *kos* is a police-station. The police are thieves and extortioners . . . but at least they do not suffer any rivals. All castes and kinds of men move here . . . Brahmins and chumris, bankers and tinkers, barbers and bunnias, pilgrims and potters—all the world going and coming.

Out of the Grand Trunk Road, Miriam, the wife of Ephraim ("Jews in Shushan") wandered in search of her dead little ones and when

the sun rose and beat upon her head, . . . she turned into the cool wet crops to lie down, and never came back.

In "Route Marchin'," the Regiment is marching along the Grand Trunk Road.

Oh, there's them Injian temples to admire when you see,
There's the peacock round the corner an' the monkey up the tree,
An' there's that rummy silver grass a-wavin' in the wind,
An' the old Grand Trunk a trailin' like a rifle-sling be'ind.
    While it's best foot first,
    And the road a-sliding past,
    An' every bloomin' campin'-ground exactly like the last;
    While the Big Drum says,
    With 'is "*rowdy-dowdy-dow!*"—
    "*Kiko kissywarsti* don't you *hamsher argy jow?*"

LAHORE, KIM'S CITY, A VIEW FROM THE FORT

Lahore was the City of Dreadful Night

Photograph by Brown Brothers, N. Y.

"MOTHER GUNGA"—THE GANGES RIVER

The holy river of the Hindus. For three years Findlayson (*The Bridge Builders*) had endured heat and cold, disappointment, discomfort, danger, and disease, in order to build the great Kashi bridge over the river, when the terrible flood descended

There is nothing especially striking about the town of Meridki, a few miles north of Lahore, but there lived "The Dormice" ("By Word of Mouth")—Dumoise the Civil Surgeon and his wife—who in life loved each other with absorbing devotion and who in death were most strangely united. Dumoise takes an unimportant part in "The Mark of the Beast" (*Life's Handicap*) and now we meet again Strickland of the Police, "who knows as much of the natives of India as is good for any man." When Fleete insulted the god Hanuman he received the "mark of the beast" from the Silver Man, "a leper as white as snow," who

> "had no face, because he was a leper of some years' standing, and his disease was heavy upon him";

and at Strickland's bungalow, Strickland and the Correspondent tortured the Silver Man with the red-hot gun-barrels and the tightening cord until he removed the spell and "the soul of Fleete" came "back into the eyes." Strickland and the Correspondent took part in another of India's mysteries when Strickland learned a further lesson in regard to the nature of the Oriental in his discovery behind the ceiling-cloth of the awful Thing which had once been Imray ("The Return of Imray"), the "fluttering, whispering, bolt-fumbling, lurking, loitering Someone" who, invisible to all but the wonderful dog, Tietjens, came "in the twilight to seek satisfaction."

Lahore, the capital of the Punjab, is rich with Kipling fancies. This old walled city, with its thirteen massive gates, has been of great importance since the early days of Hinduism and flourished magnificently during the reign of the Grand Moghuls. It is now the centre of art and learning of the Punjab; the Punjab University is there and the Central Museum and School of Art. Among the modern residences and public buildings, and the clanging tramcars of present-day civilization, you find the ruins of ancient palaces and Hindu temples built before the Christian era; and splendid specimens of Saracenic architecture dating from the time of Akbar and of Jehangir. The most important of these is the palace-fort of Akbar, now used as a barracks for the British Army, and known in Kipling's stories as "Fort Amara." Some of the apartments in the old palace are beautiful specimens of the favourite Saracenic decoration, pietra dura work in white marble. In "On the City Wall" (*In Black and White*), Kipling writes:

—No man knows the precise extent of Fort Amara. Three kings built it hundreds of years ago, and they say that there are miles of underground rooms beneath its walls. It is peopled with many ghosts, a detachment of Garrison Artillery, and a Company of Infantry. In its prime it held ten thousand men and filled its ditches with corpses.

Another splendid building of Saracenic architecture is the white marble tomb of Anarkali, a beautiful slave

SNAKE CHARMERS

Such sights as this Kim and the Lama saw along the Grand Trunk Road in their search for the River of Healing

girl, who was buried alive by the Emperor Akbar on suspicion that she had been unfaithful to him with his son Jehangir, who afterward erected the tomb and inscribed thereon in Persian the lines:

> "Ah, if I could again see the face of my beloved,
> To the day of judgment I would give thanks to my creator."

Zam-Zammeh meaning, "the lion's roar," is the name of the great gun which stands near the old Art Museum and which figured for generations in the wars of the Punjab. Lahore was Kim's home, and our first glimpse of Kim is playing king-of-the-castle astride Zam-Zammeh, that "fire-breathing dragon," the great green-bronze piece "which is always first of the conqueror's loot." Here he meets the lama and here begins their pilgrimage in search of the River of the Arrow and the Red Bull on a Green Field. Close by, in the Art Museum, the lama and the curator of the museum, the original of whom is supposed to be Mr. Lockwood Kipling, discussed the wonders and beauties of the Buddhist religion, and Kim lay with his ear to the door to learn the mission of the lama. Near the walls of the city is the beautiful Mosque of Wazir Khan from whose tall minaret the restless observer gazed out over Lahore City on a stifling August night:

Doré might have drawn it! Zola could describe it—this spectacle of sleeping thousands in the moonlight and in the shadow of the

Moon. The roof-tops are crammed with men, women and children and the air is full of undistinguishable noises. They are restless in the City of Dreadful Night; and small wonder. The marvel is that they can even breathe. If you gaze intently at the multitude, you can see that they are almost as uneasy as a daylight crowd; but the tumult is subdued. Everywhere, in the strong light, you can watch the sleepers turning to and fro; shifting their beds and again resettling them. In the pit-like court-yards of the houses there is the same movement.

The pitiless Moon shows it all.

Within a hundred yards of the Mosque of Wazir Khan stood the opium den, "The Gate of the Hundred Sorrows" (*Plain Tales from the Hills*), where the Eurasian Gabral Misquitta, who cared for nothing in the world but the "Black Smoke," lay on his mat in a corner and smoked day and night, "quiet, soothed, and contented," while murder and hideous death and wickedness of all sorts took place in his very sight.

The bazars of Lahore are thoroughly old-world and Oriental. The hot, narrow streets reek with the indescribable odour of native India, an oppressive but not altogether disagreeable combination of cheap tobacco, rancid butter, garlic, onions, currie powder, and cocoanut oil with roses, jasmine, spices, and musk. The shopkeepers lounge lazily amid their wares piled up on the floor of their little box-like stalls, and the gaunt pariah dogs sniff here and there in their occupation of city scavengers.

Copyright by Underwood & Underwood, N. Y.

A NATIVE BAZAAR AT LAHORE

In one of these bazaars Kim, by reason of his Irish blandishments, and his rout of the Brahminee bull, won from the low-caste vegetable seller a warm meal for himself and his Lama

It was in the Motee Bazar that the good-natured, low-caste vegetable-seller gave Kim his first meal for the lama. Far out near the railway station is the Kashmir Serai, the scene of Kim's first move in the Great Game, when Mahbub Ali bade him carry to Umballa "the pedigree of the white stallion." The Kashmir Serai is a

huge open square over against the railway station, surrounded with arched cloisters where the camel and horse caravans put up on their return from Central Asia. Here were all manner of Northern folk, tending tethered ponies and kneeling camels; loading and unloading bales and bundles; drawing water for the evening meal at the creaking well windlasses; piling grass before the shrieking, wild-eyed stallions; cuffing the surly caravan dogs; paying off camel drivers; taking on new grooms; swearing, shouting, arguing, and chaffering in the packed square. The cloisters, reached by three or four masonry steps, made a haven of refuge around this turbulent sea. Most of them were rented to traders, as we rent the arches of a viaduct; the space between pillar and pillar being bricked or boarded off into rooms, which were guarded by heavy wooden doors and cumbrous native padlocks.

The home of "William the Conqueror" (*The Day's Work*) and of Scott of the Irrigation Department was in Lahore. There during a dinner at the Martyns', Scott began to feel a very deep interest in William the Conqueror, the

girl who never set foot on the ground if a horse were within hail; who rode to dances with a shawl thrown over her skirt; who wore her hair cropped and curling all over her head; who answered in-

> differently to the name of William or Bill; whose speech was heavy with the flowers of the vernacular; who could act in amateur theatricals, play on the banjo, rule eight servants and two horses, their accounts and their diseases, and look men slowly and deliberately between the eyes—even after they had proposed to her and been rejected.

Thus began the little drama which had its climax when, in the midst of their splendid work among the famine-stricken people of the Madras Presidency, William the Conqueror saw Scott at the head of his procession of famine babies and milch goats and

> beheld with new eyes a young man, beautiful as Paris, a god in a halo of golden dust, walking slowly at the head of his flocks, while at his knee ran small naked Cupids.

And the happy end of the drama came during Christmas week in Lahore—the time of greatest festivity in the Punjab—when William and Scott celebrated their homecoming; and William found herself

> "unofficially . . . the chief and honoured guest among the Stewards, who could make things very pleasant for their friends."

In Lahore, lived Lalun ("On the City Wall") who was

> "beautiful exceedingly according to the native standards which are practically the same as those of the West":

AMRITSAR—THE GOLDEN TEMPLE

At Amritsar, Kim, by his clever trickery, won the ticket to Umballa from the Amritsar "Breaker of Hearts," and here took place William the Conqueror's informal little tea-party on the train. Lieutenant Golightly's humiliation occurred at Amritsar

and at the window of her house on the city wall she sang to her *sitar* patriotic native songs which helped to rouse in the breast of Khem Singh, the captive at Fort Amara, his slumbering hatred of the English and the memory of days when he was

> "a great man . . . who had once made history with a thousand followers, and would have been princeling but for the power of the Supreme Government."

During the Mohorrum riots at Lahore between Mussulman and Hindu, Wali Dad, the young Mahomedan, carried away by his fierce, racial instincts, which he thought had died within him, plunged into the fight and forgot his promise to help Lalun in a certain conspiracy; and it was at Lalun's house that the Correspondent, in helping Khem Singh to escape, became an innocent party to that conspiracy, thus proving true Lalun's declaration that the Correspondent would one day become her vizier.

The "great, red-walled city" told of in "Without Benefit of Clergy" (*Life's Handicap*) as the home of Ameera, was probably Lahore. There in the little native house, far removed from his English bungalow and its life, John Holden of the Civil Service and Ameera, a Mussulman's daughter whom he had bought from her mother, lived with their baby son, "a gold-coloured little god," a life whose "delight was too perfect to endure"; and which ended so sorrowfully when sickness smote to death both the baby son and Ameera, and John Holden, leaning above the girl who was "all but all the world in his eyes," caught her last whisper:

> "I bear witness—I bear witness . . . that there is no God but—thee, beloved!"

The romance of Trejago and Bisesa ("Beyond the Pale") was probably also a romance of Lahore. In the heart of the native city Trejago, an Englishman, stumbled on Bisesa, a daughter of India, "fairer than bar-gold in the mint," and learned to love her "more than anyone else in the world" and to find her "an endless delight," until the blissful idyll ended abruptly with the terrible punishment suffered by Bisesa for her stolen love-feast, and her mysterious and complete disappearance from the life of her English lover.

Just out of Lahore is the jungle near the Bridge of Boats over the Ravi River which was a favourite place of meeting of the four friends, Mulvaney, Learoyd, Ortheris, and the Correspondent, when they were freed for a few hours from duty at "Fort Amara." It was in one of the pontoons of the Bridge of Boats that Mulvaney, dabbling his bare toes in the water, after being "walked off" by his two chums, Learoyd and Ortheris, fully repented of his wish to shoot Sergeant Mullins who had insulted him; and, drinking the Correspondent's beer, talked himself into good humour again with the story of "Black Jack" (*Soldiers Three*), which told of Sergeant O'Hara, who was threatened with murder by

THE SUTTEE PILLAR AT BENARES

The English have now forbidden this terrible custom. *The Last Suttee* tells of the Rajput queen who, by means of her disguise as a dancing girl, eluded the palace guards and found the death she sought on the funeral pyre of the king.

the Black Tyrone and saved by Mulvaney's neat little trick with the Martini Henri rifle. In the tall grass of this jungle, Lieutenant Ouless ("His Private Honour"), the young Subaltern who had thoughtlessly struck with his cane Private Ortheris—"a good man, a proved man, and an Englishman"—retrieved his error by giving full satisfaction with the fists to the insulted private and won his warm commendation: "There ain't nothing wrong with Ouless. 'E's a gentleman all over!" Near the same spot took place the violent struggle of Ortheris's soul ("The Madness of Private Ortheris") when, lying "on his stomach with his head between his fists, . . . he swore quietly into the blue sky"; went "mad with the homesickness"; "waded through the deep waters of affliction and behaved abominably."

The military cantonment of Lahore is Mian Mir, two or three miles to the southeast, the most dreary, desolate, unhealthful cantonment in the whole of India.

The Regiment of Stanley Ortheris was stationed at Mian Mir when the Special Correspondent saved Stanley from punishment for being "drunk and disorderly" and, much against his will, received from Stanley, as a hostage for his future good behaviour, the dog he loved best in the world ("Garm—A Hostage"),

——a dog with whom one lives alone for at least six months in the year; a free thing, tied to you so strictly by love that without you he will not stir or exercise; a patient, temperate, humorous, wise soul who knows your moods before you know them yourself, is not a dog under any ruling.

Then there was no peace or happiness for the Correspondent, annoyed and uncomfortable at the pain he was involuntarily causing: for the Correspondent's dog, Vixen, hurt and jealous because of her master's attention to the strange dog; or for Stanley or his dog who were breaking their hearts over the separation from each other; until the Correspondent set out with Garm and Vixen and at last found Stanley in the Hills, where he had been sent on sick leave. At sight of his master Garm

flew through the air bodily, and I heard the whack of him as he flung himself at Stanley, knocking the little man clean over. They rolled on the ground together, shouting and yelping and hugging. I could not see which was dog and which was man,

and Stanley decided that "he was not going to give up Garm any more to anybody under the rank of Beelzebub." So the Correspondent and Stanley and Garm and Vixen became "the four happiest people in all the world that night."

If, like Kim and the lama, you take the night train from Lahore, you come to "the fort-like railway station, black in the end of night"—Lahore is an important military command and the railroad station is built so that it may be used as a fort if need be—and see what Kim and the lama saw—"the electrics sizzling over the goods yard where day and night they handle the heavy northern traffic," and the

> gigantic stone hall paved, it seemed, with the sheeted dead—third-class passengers who had taken their tickets overnight and were sleeping in the waiting-rooms. All hours of the twenty-four are alike to Orientals, and their passenger traffic is regulated accordingly—

then, when the train roars in, the sleepers springing to life

> and the station filled with clamour and shoutings, cries of water and sweetmeat vendors, shouts of native policemen, and shrill yells of women gathering up their baskets, their families, and their husbands.

About thirty miles down the line from Lahore lies Amritsar where by his clever trickery, Kim won the ticket to Umballa from the Amritsar "Breaker of Hearts"; and where took place William the Conqueror's informal little tea-party on the train.

The walled city of Amritsar, one of the most important cities of the Punjab, is remarkably beautiful with its magnificent palaces, graceful towers, and green parks. Founded in the middle of the sixteenth century, it has always been the capital city of the Sikhs. Here Ranjit Singh, the great Sikh leader, who at one time owned the Koh-i-Noor diamond, built the Golden Temple, which stands on a marble platform in the midst of a clear blue lake, "The Pool of Immortality." The lower parts of the walls are of white marble, but all the rest of the building is covered with gilded copper and the four doors are plated with silver. Inside on a white silk sheet sits, day and night, one of the priests of the Sikhs, in the midst of votive offerings of flowers and grain and money, reading the *Granth*, the holy book of the Sikhs, while peacock fans are waved above his head and his pupils gather about him, listening to his words. Hundreds of fearless doves, cooing and fluttering here and there, complete the impressive scene.

Lieutenant Golightly's humiliation ("The Arrest of Lieutenant Golightly") occurred at Amritsar. It was while Golightly was riding down from Dalhousie to Pathankote that a heavy rainstorm so ruined his spick and span riding costume that from having the appearance of "an Officer and a Gentleman"—"If there was one thing on which Golightly prided himself more than another, it was looking like an Officer and a Gentleman"—he came to look like a "most villainous loafer." It was not surprising, then, that he was arrested on suspicion of being a private who had deserted; and, although he fought and raged and "swore won'erful" until he was "nearly hysterical," he was ignominiously carried in custody to Amritsar and released only when one of his own majors appeared and, after making due allowances, recognized him as the proverbially immaculate Golightly.

At Umballa, a military station containing nothing of

particular interest to the tourist, the traveller changes cars from the Northwestern to the East Indian Railway. Not far from Umballa, little Shadd, Mulvaney's only child, died almost before he had breathed, as if in fulfilment of the "Black Curse of Shielygh," hurled at Mulvaney by old Mother Sheehy ("The Courtship of Dinah Shadd"); and thus came the "inextinguishable sorrow" of Mulvaney and his Dinah Shadd, "the strong, the patient, and the infinitely tender."

At Umballa, Kim and the lama spent a peaceful night at the home of the cultivator's relatives, and Kim delivered to Creighton Sahib "the white stallion's pedigree."

Saharanpur is a small town, but is well worth visiting for the sake of its fine botanical gardens and its splendid view of the Himalaya Mountains. At Saharanpur was the "long white rambling house" where the old woman from Kulu—"a woman with a heart of gold but a talker—something of a talker—" entertained with such cordial hospitality Kim and the lama and Hurree Babu; cared for the lama during Kim's sickness, and, with all a mother's tenderness, nursed Kim back to health. It was near this home at Saharanpur that the lama found at last his River of the Arrow, and freed Kim from the "Wheel of Things."

". . . the River of the Arrow is here . . . I have found it. Son of my soul, I have wrenched my soul back from the Threshold of Freedom to free thee from all sin—as I am free, and sinless. Just is the Wheel. Certain is our deliverance. Come!"

He crossed his hands on his lap and smiled, as a man may who has won Salvation for himself and his beloved.

When Kim, restless with the routine of St. Xavier's, "ran out to learn the game alone," he came to Delhi in the course of his wanderings and pronounced it "a wonderful city." He spoke none too strongly. For forty-five square miles about the site of present-day Delhi lie the ruins of former Delhis. One Moghul emperor after another, dissatisfied with the location of the capital, built a new city near the old one until, in all, six or seven cities have risen to power and fallen to decay in practically the same location. The Delhi of to-day was founded in 1631 by Shah Jehan, that emperor lover who is best known as the builder of the peerless Taj Mahal at Agra.

Inside the walls of the palace fort are pavilions and closed apartments in bewildering profusion. Of chief interest are the Pearl Mosque of white and gray marble exquisitely carved and inlaid with mother-of-pearl, and the Halls of Public and Private Audience, dazzling in their gorgeous beauty of carved white marble inlaid with gold and gems and semi-precious stones. The Hall of Private Audience is said to be the most beautiful single apartment in the world; and here we read, inscribed in Persian on the walls, the frequently-quoted lines:

> If heaven can be on the face of the earth,
> It is this, oh! it is this, oh! it is this!

THE BRIDGE OF BOATS OVER THE HOOGHLY RIVER AT CALCUTTA

Somewhere here was Fultah Fisher's boarding-house, "where sailor men reside," where Hans, the blue-eyed Dane, was slain by Salem Hardieker, and where Anne of Austria looted the Maid Ultruda's charm, "the little silver crucifix that keeps a man from harm"

In the Hall of Public Audience once stood the wonderful Peacock Throne, a massive structure wrought of gold and priceless gems.

From the Lahore Gate in the Fort to the Lahore Gate in the city wall runs the Chandni Chauk, one of the best-known streets in the world. A macadamized road a mile long and one hundred and twenty feet broad, and lined with noble trees, it is the busiest street in India and the gayest and most diversified in colour and type. The best shops in Delhi are there, and the constant procession of men on the backs of elephants and camels and horses, riding in palanquins or carriages, or walking along the street, make up one of the most interesting scenes in the Orient.

The chief reminder of the prominent part which Delhi took in the Sepoy Rebellion is the battered Kashmir Gate which speaks so eloquently of the almost unbelievable heroism of Brigadier-General John Nicholson and his men.

The Jama Masjid, or Great Mosque, of red sandstone and white marble, should certainly be visited; and an eleven-mile drive carries one out to the Kutb Minar, that shaft of red sandstone and white marble, richly carved and gracefully shaped, which inspired Bishop Heber's praise:

"The Moghuls designed like Titans and finished like jewellers."

After the disastrous defeat of Paniput, Scindia, the

Mahratta chief ("With Scindia to Delhi"), with "Lalun," a maid he loved, lashed behind him on his horse, fled to Delhi pursued by an Afghan,

> "A swine-fed reiver of the North that lusted for the maid."

Close to the city walls, Scindia's horse became exhausted with the double burden—

> Yea, Delhi town was very near when Lalun whispered: "Slay!
> "Lord of my life, the mare sinks fast—stab deep and let me die!"
> But Scindia would not, and the maid tore free and flung away,
> And turning as she fell we heard the clattering Populzai.
>
> . . . .
>
> Our Gods were kind. Before he heard the maiden's piteous scream,
> A log upon the Delhi road, beneath the mare he lay—
> Lost mistress and lost battle passed before him like a dream;
> The darkness closed about his eyes—I bore my King away.

At Cawnpore we change cars for Lucknow, for, although Lucknow is somewhat off the regular line, we turn aside to visit the city where Kim went "up to the Gates of Learning." Lucknow is the scene of the famous siege in the Mutiny, of which the ruined Residency, with the "banner of England" always flying from "the topmost roof," is a pathetic monument. The city, once the capital of Oude, is comparatively modern, with wide, beautiful parks scattered here and there and great buildings ornately decorated—a city of kings, all green and white and gold. In the old days, the gates of the public parks were set with jewels, and one of the streets was paved with silver. The great Imambara, in which stood the silver throne, bears witness to the magnificence of the Kings of Oude. The Great Imambara, built for a shrine in which to celebrate the Mahorrum, the famous Mahomedan New Year's festival, is a most imposing structure, with vast halls of tesselated marble surrounding an open court. Another building, especially noticeable, is the Chutter Munzil, once the king's harem, now used as a Club House and Public Library, whose great domes look like golden umbrellas. A drive through Lucknow, seeing what Kim saw from his *ticca-gharri*, and we heartily endorse Kim's words, "a fair city—a beautiful city!"

> There is no city—except Bombay, the queen of all—more beautiful in her garish style than Lucknow, whether you see her from the bridge over the river, or the top of the Imambara, looking down on the gilt umbrellas of the Chutter Munzil, and the trees in which the town is bedded. Kings have adorned her with fantastic buildings, endowed her with charities, crammed her with pensioners, and drenched her with blood. She is the centre of all idleness, intrigue, and luxury, and shares with Delhi the claim to talk the only pure Urdu.

Lucknow was Hannasyde's station ("On the Strength of a Likeness") and when Mrs. Landys-Haggert stopped off at Lucknow to attend a big ball at the Chutter Munzil, Hannasyde continued the attentions he had shown to her at Simla a month previous, because she was like his old sweetheart, Alice Chisane, who had married another man. And here Mrs. Haggert bade him farewell:

> As the train went out slowly, Mrs. Landys-Haggert leaned out of the window to say good-bye—"On second thoughts *au revoir*, Mr. Hannasyde. I go Home in the Spring, and perhaps I may meet you in town."
>
> Hannasyde shook hands, and said very earnestly and adoringly —"I hope to Heaven I shall never see your face again!"
>
> And Mrs. Haggert understood.

Coming back to Cawnpore, one of the chief manufacturing cities of India, the traveller turns at once to the memorials of the city's tragic part in the Great Mutiny of 1857. Chief of these memorials is Marochetti's marble statue of the Angel of the Resurrection surrounded by a Gothic screen in the midst of a delightful park. Over the gate of the screen are inscribed the words, "These are they which came out of great tribulation"; and on the pedestal of the statue,

> Sacred to the perpetual Memory of the great company of Christian people, chiefly Women and Children, who near this spot were cruelly massacred by the followers of the rebel Nana Doondoo, Panth of Bithoor, and cast, the dying with the dead, into the well below, on the xvth day of July, MDCCCLVII.

Through the streets of Cawnpore Mulvaney clung to the back of a maddened elephant ("My Lord, the

CALCUTTA

Me, the Sea-captain loved, the river built;
   Wealth sought and Kings adventured life to hold.
Hail, England! I am Asia—Power on silt,
   Death in my hands, but gold!

—*The Song of the Cities*

Elephant") and, by punishment and kindness wisely mingled, conquered the great beast and won his friendship; so that years afterward on the Frontier the elephant refused to go forward with his guns—thus blocking the Pass and delaying the advance of two thousand soldiers—until he had seen his old friend Mulvaney.

"Down, Malachi," I sez, "an' put me up . . ." He was on his knees in a minut an' he slung me up as gentle as a girl. "Go on, now, my son," I sez. "You're blockin' the road." He fetched wan more joyous toot, an' swung grand out av the head av the Tangi, his gun-spear clankin' on his back, an' at the back av him there wint the most amazin' shout I iver heard.

Now is sighted the Ganges River, which flows from the Himalaya Mountains fifteen hundred miles to the Bay of Bengal. This is the holy river of the Hindus who swear "by the waters of the Ganges," as Christians take their oath by the Bible. "Mother Gunga," as the Hindus call her, is believed to spring from the feet of Vishnu and to cleanse from all sin. For three years, Findlayson ("The Bridge-builders") "had endured heat and cold, disappointment, discomfort, danger, and disease, with responsibility almost too heavy for one pair of shoulders," in order to build the great Kashi Bridge over the Ganges, when the terrible flood descended which almost wrecked his honour and happiness, for "there were no excuses in his service. Government might listen perhaps, but his own kind would judge him by his bridge, as that stood or fell."

Then came the grumbling of Mother Gunga because the bridge-builders had her in irons, and the council of the gods from which Mother Gunga retired baffled and beaten, and Findlayson emerged triumphant, for his beloved bridge held firm.

Benares, where, at the Temple of the Tirthankers, the lama made his home when Kim was not with him, was founded three thousand years ago and is the holiest of holy cities, for it is sacred to Buddhists as well as Hindus (at the beginning of his teachings, Buddha came to Benares), some seven hundred million people in all. The Hindu believes that while the rest of the world rests on the back of a tortoise, Benares is upheld on the trident of Vishnu, the god of preservation, who further blessed the city with a well thirty feet deep, filled with his own perspiration, by bathing in which a man receives an absolute surety of heaven. This well is a revolting mixture of stagnant water and decayed flowers and foodstuffs which have been thrown in as religious offerings by the thousands of Hindus who go down the steps of the well to drink and bathe in the water. Among the hundreds of temples and mosques at Benares, the only one of real beauty is the Mosque of Aurungzebe with its two slender, graceful minarets towering high above the city. The brass work and silks of the bazaars will de-

A TEMPLE OF THE TIRTHANKERS AT BENARES

In a cell here the Lama made his home when Kim was not with him, and here Kim cured the Jat's child of a fever

tain the traveller for a time, but he will soon leave the arcaded, tortuous streets, narrow and filthy, where the sacred cows and monkeys are allowed full liberty, for the riverside, the chief attraction of Benares. The best way to see this is to sit in a comfortable chair on the deck of a river boat which the coolies row slowly up and down. For three miles the high bank swarms with palaces, temples, mosques, and long flights of steps going up from the river at every point. Here, among the sacred cattle and the pariah dogs, congregate the Hindus engaged in the ceremonies of their religion—priests under their huge umbrellas; wild-eyed, self-torturing fakirs, naked and loathsome in grease and paint and ashes; and countless devotees bathing in the river, which receives the sewage of the city, or burning their dead on its banks. No wonder Kim thought Benares, "a peculiarly filthy city."

To the temple of Prithi-Devi in Benares ("The Incarnation of Krishna Mulvaney"), the coolies carried Mulvaney in the gorgeous palanquin which "the three musketeers" had won in fair fight from Dearsley, foreman of the construction works; and from the shelter of the palanquin Mulvaney saw, at the big Queens' Praying in the temple, the wives and daughters, of most of the kings of India,

more glorious than thransformations at a pantomime, for they was in pink an' blue an' silver an' red an' grass green, wid di'monds an' im'ralds an' great red rubies all over thim. But that was the least part av the glory . . . they were more lovely than the like av any loveliness in hivin; ay, their little bare feet were better than the white hands av a lord's lady, an' their mouths were like puckered roses, an' their eyes were bigger and dharker than the eyes av any livin' women I've seen.

There, wrapping the pink lining of his palanquin around him for a mantle, and using a beer bottle for a flute, Mulvaney impersonated the god Krishna before the worshipful, credulous gaze of the women, and thus escaped from the temple.

Now the train speeds through Bengal toward Calcutta, and the climate and the scenery change completely. The air is heavy and moist, and fragrant with the flowers and spicy weeds of the tropical woodland. All nature riots in luxuriance of growth and loveliness of colour, and the forests on both sides of the track are wide and deep with a vast amount of tangled undergrowth. Far to the east are the beautiful wooded mountains of Assam where, among the Garo Hills, Kala Nag (*The Jungle Book*) carried little Toomai to the elephant dance. Off in the west are the Seonee Hills, the home of Mowgli (*The Jungle Book*) and his wolf brothers, who conquered Tabaqui, the cowardly jackal, and Shere Khan, the wicked, man-eating tiger, and years later drove at their will the guilty Abdul Gafur and the Nilghai, and taught Gisborne of the Woods and Forests and

THE SHWE DAGON PAGODA

In *The Song of the Cities,* Rangoon greets England with the words,

"Hail, Mother. Do they call me rich in trade?
Little care I, but hear the shorn priest drone,
And watch my silk-clad lovers, man by maid,
Laugh 'neath my Shwe Dagon."

Muller, his Chief, strange secrets of "The Rukh" (*Many Inventions*).

Not many miles from the Seonee Hills are the Satpura Hills, the "scrubby, tigerish country," where John Chinn, the Second ("The Tomb of his Ancestors"), the young Subaltern whom the Bhils believed to be the reincarnation of his own grandfather, brought his "hereditary influence" to bear in vaccinating the frightened community; and by shooting his beautiful "tiger horse," put a stop to the ghostly night rides which had so terrorized the little black people of the hills.

Calcutta, lying on the "sullen, un-English stream, the Hooghly," was, until the recent change to Delhi, the capital of British India. To enter Calcutta from Benares, the traveller goes into Howrah and crosses the Hooghly River with its wonderful pontoon bridge and its immense and varied shipping. The city of Calcutta is thoroughly cosmopolitan, all nations of the East and West mingling in her streets. The traveller will find the general sights of interest of every large city, fine public buildings, statues, monuments, and parks; while the white, spacious mansions of the Europeans in their beautiful gardens of tropical plants facing the broad boulevards, completely overshadow in the general view the narrow, dirty streets of native Bengal, and give the city an air of luxuriant wealth hard to equal anywhere else in the world. This impression of luxury is especially striking at sunset when the richly appointed turn-outs roll down the Chowringhee Road and along the wide Esplanade by the river where the military band plays its gayest music and everybody is dressed in the latest mode. Three or four miles from the city are the magnificent botanical gardens—the finest in the world—where, among rare and wonderfully beautiful plants, is the famous Great Banyan under which a thousand people might easily find shelter. The story of Calcutta is briefly told in "The Song of the Cities":

> Me, the Sea-captain loved, the river built;
> Wealth sought and Kings adventured life to hold.
> Hail, England! I am Asia—Power on silt,
> Death in my hands, but gold!

"The God-forgotten City of Calcutta" is what Duncan Parrenness, Writer to the Most Honourable the East India Company ("The Dream of Duncan Parrenness"), calls the old capital when he writes from Calcutta in the days of Warren Hastings:

> . . . and I saw how the one year that I had lived in this land had so burned and seared my mind with the flames of a thousand bad passions and desires that I had aged ten months for each one in the Devil's school;

and goes on to tell of his distressing vision when his "trust in man," his "faith in women," and his "boy's soul and conscience" were lost to him forever.

At Fultah Fisher's boarding-house in Calcutta ("The

Ballad of Fisher's Boarding-House") Salem Hardieker, the "lean Bostonian," because of the lies told him by his Light-o'-Love, Anne of Austria, murdered "Hans, the Blue-eyed Dane,"

> Bull-throated, bare of arm,
> Who carried on his hairy chest
> The maid Ultruda's charm—
> The little silver crucifix
> That keeps a man from harm.

It was at Calcutta cantonments that the Eurasian lady ("Private Learoyd's Story") coveted the fox terrier belonging to the Colonel's wife and was tricked by Mulvaney, Learoyd, and Ortheris, who won the money reward and at the same time saved to the Colonel's lady her precious "Rip."

VII
ON THE ROAD TO MANDALAY

VII

On the Road to Mandalay

IT is of Burma and his Burma sweetheart that the British soldier sings in "Mandalay,"

> I've a neater, sweeter maiden
> In a cleaner, greener land.

The vast mountain-ranges and dense forests of northwestern Burma forbid an overland entry from India; but well-appointed steamships of the British India lines run three times weekly from Calcutta to Rangoon, a distance of seven hundred and fifty-eight miles. One of these steamships takes the traveller speedily and comfortably across the Bay of Bengal and thirty miles up the Rangoon River to Rangoon. In "The Song of the Cities," Rangoon greets England with the words,

> Hail, Mother. Do they call me rich in trade?
> Little care I, but hear the shorn priest drone,
> And watch my silk-clad lovers, man by maid,
> Laugh 'neath my Shwe Dagon.

The object of chief interest in Rangoon is the famous Shwe Dagon Pagoda. This temple or reliquary is built over eight hairs of Buddha and relics of the former Buddhas, and is a solid mass of pyramidal masonry covered with gold leaf from base to apex and rising three hundred and seventy feet in the air from the summit of Thehngoottara Hill. Crowning the pagoda is a golden umbrella ringed and fringed with golden bells and set with diamonds, emeralds, and rubies. The clappers of the bells are flattened and elongated so that they catch the wind and keep up a continuous musical tinkling, which the Nats, the guardian angels of the Burmese, are supposed to hear and note that an act of devotion has been performed. At the base of the pagoda on every side are chapels containing massive carved figures of Buddha; and scattered here and there over the huge platform on which the pagoda stands are small pagodas of richly carved wood, or glass mosaic, or masonry covered with gold leaf like the Shwe Dagon itself; stone altars for the offerings of devotees; stalls for the sale of religious offerings; bells of all sizes; and everywhere, figures of creatures half lion and half man. These lions are symbolical of a Burmese legend which tells of a Burmese prince lost in the jungle and mothered by a lioness who, when her foster son escaped from her by swimming across a river, died of a broken heart. So the lions are a memorial of the loving devotion of the lion mother.

To the traveller it is a surprise to find in the streets of Rangoon, thronged with Americans, Europeans, Indians,

Copyright by Underwood & Underwood, N. Y.

LUCKNOW—GREAT IMAMBARAH

The city where Kim went "up to the Gates of Learning"

Copyright by H. C. White Company, N. Y.

BURMA ELEPHANT

Elephints a-pilin teak
  In the sludgy, spudgy creek,
Where the silence 'ung that 'eavy you was 'arf
    afraid to speak!   —*Mandalay*

Chinese, and Japanese, so few Burmese. In their big bazaars and at Shwe Dagon Pagoda they are seen in their true element. The women of Burma are free and respected and take an equal part with the men in all matters of life; marriage is an affair of the heart; children are adored; and the soil is lavish in its fruitfulness. It is said that for these reasons the Burmese are the happiest people on earth. It is not hard to believe this when one hears the merry talk and laughter and sees the bright faces and care-free, indolent air of these little brown people who are decked with fragrant flowers and clad in silk of the gayest colours, pink, scarlet, green, yellow, and magenta. Their flattened features show their relation to the Mongolian; and always in the mouth, whether of man, woman, or child, you see the big cheroot, for the Burmese baby learns to smoke when it learns to walk.

Almost as interesting as the Shwe Dagon Pagoda—but in quite a different way—are the timber yards where the elephants act as coolies:

> Elephints a-pilin' teak
> In the sludgy, squdgy creek.

The clear-eyed intelligence of the great beasts in lifting and stacking in regular order the logs of teak, one log often weighing more than a ton, is wonderful. Watching the "foreman elephant" pushing the log into its exact place, one almost believes the story which some one nearby is sure to tell, that he frequently squints one eye to see that the log lies true.

Burma has a railway from Rangoon through to Mandalay and beyond, but for the best view of the charming Irrawaddy River, the traveller should go from Rangoon to Mandalay by one of the boats of the Irrawaddy Flotilla Company. The steamers have three decks and the bow of the second deck is reserved for Europeans. Here the traveller may have his dining-table set, and from a steamer chair watch in perfect comfort the surrounding scenes. The odd river craft first attract the attention. Among steam tugs, rafts, barges, houseboats, and fishing boats, is seen the peculiarly curved Burmese boat guided by an oarsman who sits in an elaborately carved chair high above the stern; and speeding before the wind are the little *peingaws* carrying sails one hundred and thirty feet long. The low-lying country of the Irrawaddy Estuary is soon left behind, and now the hills and woods give to the scene a constant variety of interest and delight. All along the way, on every rise of ground, stand the monasteries of the yellow-robed Buddhist monks or dozens of white pagodas with gilded peaks and tinkling bells. It is considered an act of great merit to build a pagoda of whatever size or material; hence the enormous number throughout Burma. Here and there is a town of considerable size or a little village of quaint bamboo houses on stilts, where the rice fields almost dazzle with their vivid green and where giant palm trees reach upward toward the

BENARES
To Kim's thinking "a peculiarly filthy city"

"BY THE OLD MOULMEIN PAGODA"

"THE TINKLY TEMPLE BELLS"

"For the temple-bells are callin', an' it's there
that I would be—
By the old Moulmein Pagoda, looking lazy all
the sea."

—*Mandalay*

sun. Then the forest trees crowd close to the edge of the stream; bright-plumaged birds flutter among the branches; green monkeys gambol on the river banks; and farther back in the quiet depths the wild elephant, the rhinoceros, and the tiger have their haunts. A feature of peculiar charm in the scenery of the Irrawaddy is the frequent occurrence of flowering trees, whose boughs, laden with blossoms or leaves of crimson or scarlet or gold, shine through the rich green of the woodland with splendid effect.

In "The Taking of Lungtungpen" (*Plain Tales from the Hills*), Mulvaney, with Lieutenant Brazenose and his men, stripped and swam the Irrawaddy River that dark night when, not having time to dress again, they captured the town of Lungtungpen just as they were—"nakid as Vanus"—and so easily that the Burmese headman asked the Interpreter, "Av the English fight like that wid their clo'es off, what in the wurruld do they do wid their clo'es on?" Farther up the river at Bhamo was the cozy little home of "Georgie Porgie" (*Life's Handicap*) and "Georgina," his Burmese sweetheart who was

> "in every way as sweet and merry and honest and winning a little woman as the most exacting of bachelors could have desired."

It was from Bhamo that Georgina followed Georgie Porgie in the long and faithful search which ended so bitterly for her.

The Bride and the Bridegroom came out into the veranda after dinner, in order that the smoke of Georgie Porgie's cheroot might not hang in the new drawing-room curtains. "What is that noise down there?" said the Bride. Both listened.

"Oh," said Georgie Porgie, "I suppose some brute of a hillman has been beating his wife."

. . . .

But it was Georgina, crying, all by herself, down the hillside, among the stones of the water-course where the washermen wash the clothes.

Somewhere here in the wilds of Upper Burma lies the rebel village of "Pabengmay" ("The Grace of the Hundred Head") where Subadar Prag Tewarri, of the First Shikaris, so terribly avenged the murder of his beloved leader and piled on the grave of the young Subaltern the heads of a hundred of his enemies, to teach the Burmans "the price of a white man slain."

They made a pile of their trophies
  High as a tall man's chin,
Head upon head distorted,
  Clinched in a sightless grin,
Anger and pain and terror
  Writ on the smoke-scorched skin.

. . . . .

Then a silence came to the river,
  A hush fell over the shore,
And Bohs that were brave departed,
  And Sniders squibbed no more;
  For the Burman said
  That a *kullah's* head
Must be paid for with heads five score.

THE IRRAWADDY RIVER

In *The Taking of Lungtungpen* (*Plain Tales from the Hills*), Mulvaney with Lieutenant Brazenose and his men, stripped and swam the Irrawaddy River that dark night when, not having time to dress again, they captured the town of Lungtungpen just as they were—"nakid as Vanus." Farther up the river at Bhamo was the cozy little home of "Georgie Porgie" (*Life's Handicap*) and "Georgina," his Burmese sweetheart

ON THE ROAD TO MANDALAY

There's a widow in sleepy Chester
Who weeps for her only son;
There's a grave on the Pabeng River,
A grave that the Burmans shun,
And there's Subudar Prag Tewarri
Who tells how the work was done.

Off to the west lies the Chindwin River, where took place the scrimmages between the Burman Boh Da Thone,

"Erst a pretender to Thebaw's Throne"

("The Ballad of Boh Da Thone"), and the dauntless Captain O'Neil, with his "Black Tyrone" regiment,

the choicest collection of unmitigated blackguards, dog-stealers, robbers of hen-roosts, assaulters of innocent citizens, and recklessly daring heroes in the Army List.

And there is the cart road of the Government Bullock Train where, beneath the weighty bulk of Babu Harendra Mukerji, the Boh ended his life in undignified fashion and forfeited his head which later so gruesomely interrupted Captain O'Neil's honeymoon:

Open-eyed, open-mouthed, on the napery's snow,
With a crash and a thud, rolled—the Head of the Boh!
And gummed to the scalp was a letter which ran:

In Fielding Force Service,
Encampment,
10th Jan.

Dear Sir,—I have honour to send, *as you said*,
For final approval (see under) Boh's Head;

Was took by myself in most bloody affair.
By High Education brought pressure to bear.

Now violate Liberty, time being bad,
To mail V. P. P. (rupees hundred). Please add

Whatever Your Honour can pass. Price of Blood
Much cheap at one hundred, and children want food.

So trusting Your Honour will somewhat retain
True love and affection for Govt. Bullock Train,

And show awful kindness to satisfy me,
I am,
Graceful Master,
Your
H. Mukerji.

It was way over there in the East near the Shan States that Hicksey of the Police ("A Conference of the Powers") captured Boh Naghee, the Burmese robber chief, by taking a flying leap on his head while he lay in bed under a mosquito net; and the Dacoit chased by the Infant, fell over the palisades on top of Dennis, the frightened and bewildered Civil Officer; and the whole affair ended with a little picnic of sandwiches.

The first glance at the city of Mandalay, laid out like the squares of a checker board, with good roads, good drainage, street lamps, and efficient police protection, makes one feel that he has reached a town of the Ameri-

MANDALAY—THE "FOUR HUNDRED AND FIFTY PAGODAS"

Here on Mandalay Hill sat the British Soldier and his little Burma girl, listening to the "East a-callin'" and the "tinkly temple bells"
—*Mandalay*

can western country, but the little bamboo houses and the ever-present pagodas soon dispel the illusion. In the very centre of the city stands the walled town which was once the capital of the weak King Thebaw and his cruel queen, Supaiyah Lat, who, to insure prosperity to the city in its building, and afterward to protect it from the British, caused scores of her subjects to be buried alive beneath the walls. Many years ago the Burmese monarch was deposed and sent into exile in India, and his city serves now as a fort of the British Army. But the gilded palaces of the king and his four queens still stand and the magnificent audience chambers are but little changed. Surrounding the royal city is a moat one hundred feet wide filled with water where hundreds of pink and white lotus lilies give a captivating picturesqueness to the scene. One of the "sights" of Mandalay is the series of pagodas called the "Four Hundred and Fifty Pagodas," for under each pagoda rests a marble slab engraved with one of the four hundred and fifty commandments of the Buddhist law. High above Mandalay, and almost surrounding it, rise the ruby mine mountains, and within the city itself is Mandalay Hill covered with countless pagodas. From this hill you can obtain a splendid view of the town and the surrounding country.

The journey is ended. The mist is on the rice fields and the sun is dropping slow. Here on Mandalay Hill under the palm-trees sit the British Soldier and his little

Burma girl, gazing dreamily out over the river, and listening to the "tinkly temple bells."

If you've 'eard the East a-callin', you won't never 'eed naught else.
No! you won't 'eed nothin' else
But them spicy garlic smells,
An' the sunshine an' the palm-trees an' the tinkly temple-bells;
On the Road to Mandalay,
Where the old Flotilla lay;
Can't you 'ear their paddles chunkin' from Rangoon to Mandalay,
On the Road to Mandalay,
Where the flyin'-fishes play,
An' the dawn comes up like thunder outer China 'crost the Bay!

INDEX

INDEX